The
30 MINUTE
CHEF
100
FAST RECIPES
FOR FRANTIC COOKS

The
30 MINUTE
CHEF
100
FAST RECIPES
FOR FRANTIC COOKS

BROCKHAMPTON PRESS
LONDON

First published in Great Britain in 1993 by
Anaya Publishers Ltd,
Strode House, 44–50 Osnaburgh Street, London NW1 3ND

This edition published 1996 by Brockhampton Press,
a member of Hodder Headline PLC Group

Recipes by MARY CADOGAN, JACQUELINE CLARK, CAROLE HANDSLIP and LYN RUTHERFORD
Managing Editor JANET ILLSLEY
Photography by JAMES MURPHY, ALAN NEWNHAM and CLIVE STREETER
Jacket design by EDWIN BELCHAMBER
Designer PEDRO PRÁ-LOPEZ
Food Stylists MARY CADOGAN, JACQUELINE CLARK, CAROLE HANDSLIP and LYN RUTHERFORD
Photographic Stylist SUE RUSSELL
Background Artist ANNABEL PLAYFAIR
Introduction by DEBORAH GRAY

British Library Cataloguing in Publication Data

Thirty-minute Chef: Over 100 Fast Recipes for Frantic Cooks
641.5

ISBN 1 86019 006 5

Typeset by SX Composing Ltd., Rayleigh, Essex
Colour reproduction by J. Film Process, Bangkok
Printed in UK by BPC Books Ltd

NOTES

Ingredients are listed in metric and imperial measures.
Use either set of quantities but not a mixture of both.

All spoon measures are level:
1 tablespoon = one 15 ml spoon
1 teaspoon = one 5 ml spoon

Use fresh herbs and freshly ground black pepper unless otherwise stated.

Use standard size 3 eggs unless otherwise suggested.

CONTENTS

INTRODUCTION

We demand so much from the food we eat today – it has to be attractive to the eye, challenging to the taste buds and good for the body. Our palates have been educated in the foods of different cultures and the rich variety of food on sale has widened our horizons making home cooking a much more exotic affair than our grandmothers could ever have thought possible. Our life-style also dictates that we spend very little time preparing and cooking these feasts.

These demands are not necessarily impossible to meet. Cuts of fresh meat, poultry and fish are readily available that take very little time to cook. Wonderful fruit and vegetables are now always on hand, either to supplement the meat or to form the basis of a vegetarian or salad dish. If time is really short, we can even buy some of our vegetables scrubbed and prepared for cooking. When quickly cooking vegetables, quality is of the essence. Choose produce with care, selecting only firm, blemish-free samples.

Store-cupboard food is no longer second rate and flavourless. Many frozen vegetables and fruits are of excellent quality, while canned tomatoes and beans should always be ready to hand. On the supermarket shelf there are a whole range of Italian, Indian, Mexican, and Chinese ingredients making it possible for us all to be international chefs.

Our cooking methods also help us to be efficient cooks. Fast, modern grills and hobs ensure even, quick cooking. Stir frying, once a foreign cooking method is now used to produce not only Chinese-style dishes, but adaptations of our old favourites. In addition, non-stick woks and frying pans are more convenient to care for their traditional counterparts. An essential piece of equipment is a good, sharp cook's knife to speed up preparation time, although if you are regularly preparing large quantities, a food-processor is a must. In addition, a microwave can be useful for quickly reheating meals for busy families.

Modern tastes also accept meals that require no cooking at all, salad dishes based on cold meats, canned beans or fish served with delicious, warm, crusty bread is a delight on a summer evening.

This book supplies another vital ingredient – imagination. There are excellent recipes for feeding a hungry family or for providing them with a quick snack. Entertaining friends can involve many hours of preparation and headache, but not necessarily so. There are a selection of excellent starters, main dishes and desserts that you can quickly present with confidence and pride.

A little time spent in advance planning when cooking for friends always pays dividends on the night. Writing a list of jobs to be done is a great help and ticking them off is very satisfying. Whatever the occasion, these quick and easy recipes are destined to be firm favourites.

BABY CORNS WITH PEPPER SALSA

SERVES 4

If fresh baby corn cobs are not available, use canned cobs instead for this tasty colourful dish.

50 g (2 oz) butter
500 g (1 lb) baby corn cobs

SALSA
1 large red pepper, cored, seeded and chopped
1 red chilli, seeded and chopped
1 bunch spring onions, chopped
1 large beef tomato, chopped
4 tablespoons chopped coriander
1/4 teaspoon salt
2 tablespoons chopped parsley
pepper to taste

TO GARNISH
coriander sprigs

1 To make the salsa, place the red pepper, chilli, spring onions, tomato, coriander, salt and parsley in a food processor or blender and work briefly to a finely chopped mixture. Season with pepper.

2 Melt the butter in a frying pan, add the baby corns and sauté for about 8 minutes until lightly golden and just tender.

3 Arrange the corn cobs on individual plates and add a spoonful of pepper salsa to each serving. Garnish with coriander.

GRILLED VEGETABLES WITH PESTO

SERVES 4

Take advantage of the smaller varieties of vegetables appearing in markets and supermarkets today – and treat them simply. This dish also makes a good accompaniment to roast lamb.

4 tablespoons olive oil
125 g (4 oz) baby courgettes
125 g (4 oz) baby corn
125 g (4 oz) button mushrooms
125 g (4 oz) cherry tomatoes
4 tablespoons pesto
basil leaves to garnish

1 Preheat grill to high. Toss the vegetables in 2 tablespoons olive oil and place in a single layer in the grill pan.

2 Place under the grill and cook for 4-6 minutes until the vegetables are slightly blackened, turning them as necessary.

3 Mix the pesto with the remaining olive oil.

4 Place the warm vegetables in a serving dish and drizzle with the pesto dressing. Garnish with basil leaves to serve.

SPINACH & CHICKEN SOUP

SERVES 4

You can use cooked chicken for this soup, in which case omit the groundnut oil and add the ginger, garlic and spring onions to the stock with the spinach.

250 g (8 oz) boneless chicken breast, skinned
1 tablespoon groundnut oil
1 cm (½ inch) piece fresh root ginger, chopped
2 cloves garlic, sliced
4 spring onions, diagonally sliced
900 ml (1½ pints) chicken stock
1 tablespoon soy sauce
125 g (4 oz) spinach leaves, shredded
2 tablespoons dry sherry
1 teaspoon sesame oil
salt and pepper to taste

1 Slice the chicken into very thin strips, about 2.5 cm x 5 x 5 mm (1 x ¼ x ¼ inch).

2 Heat the oil in a pan, add the chicken with the ginger, garlic and spring onions and stir fry until the chicken is sealed.

3 Put the stock into a saucepan and bring to the boil. Add the soy sauce and spinach, return to the boil and cook for 2 minutes.

4 Add the chicken mixture, sherry, sesame oil and seasoning. Heat through before serving.

COCK À LEEKIE

SERVES 4

This is a much quicker version of the famous Scottish soup which traditionally uses a capon. Leave out the prunes if you prefer.

25 g (1 oz) butter
500 g (1 lb) leeks, thinly sliced into rings
250 g (8 oz) boneless chicken breast, skinned and cut into strips
50 g (2 oz) stoneless prunes, cut into quarters
900 ml (1½ pints) chicken stock
salt and pepper to taste
1 tablespoon chopped parsley

1 Heat the butter in a pan, add the leeks and cook very gently for 10 minutes, stirring occasionally, until softened.

2 Add the chicken, prunes, stock and seasoning. Bring to the boil, cover and simmer for 15 minutes.

3 Stir in the parsley and serve.

QUICK FRIED PRAWNS WITH GINGER

SERVES 3-4

Sample these truly delicious mouthfuls of prawns with garlic, ginger and spring onion – quick fried in a light sherry batter. Serve as a starter or with rice as part of an oriental meal.

12 raw King prawns
1 teaspoon grated fresh root ginger
½ clove garlic, crushed
2 spring onions, very finely chopped
3 tablespoons self-raising flour
salt and pepper to taste
2 teaspoons sherry
1 egg, beaten
about 175 ml (6 fl oz) groundnut oil for frying
lemon wedges to garnish

1 Peel and devein the prawns, leaving the tail shells on. Place in a bowl with the ginger, garlic and spring onions; mix well.

2 Put the flour in a bowl, season and add the sherry and egg. Beat to a smooth batter. Fold in the prawns and toss to coat.

3 Heat the oil in a wok until very hot. Fry the prawns, in batches, for 2-3 minutes until golden brown and cook through. Drain on kitchen paper and keep hot while cooking the rest.

4 Transfer to a warmed serving dish and serve at once, garnished with lemon wedges.

MUSSELS IN BLACK BEAN SAUCE

SERVES 2-4

I love to eat this as a starter, scooping up the rich salty black bean sauce with the mussel shells. You can of course serve it as a main course, with rice.

750 g (1½ lb) fresh mussels
4 tablespoons sherry
2 tablespoons groundnut oil
1 clove garlic, crushed
2.5 cm (1 inch) piece fresh root ginger, grated
3 spring onions, chopped
1 teaspoon cornflour
2 tablespoons light soy sauce
½ teaspoon sugar
50 g (2 oz) canned black beans, rinsed
pepper to taste

1 Scrub the mussels thoroughly in cold water, removing their beards. Discard any with open or damaged shells.

2 Put 125 ml (4 fl oz) water in a wok or sauté pan with 2 tablespoons of the sherry and bring to the boil. Add the mussels, cover and cook for 2-3 minutes, shaking the pan once or twice, until the shells have opened. Discard any unopened mussels. Strain, reserving 6 tablespoons liquid.

3 Heat the oil in the dry wok. Add the garlic, ginger and spring onions and stir fry for 1 minute.

4 Blend the cornflour with the soy sauce, remaining sherry, sugar and mussel liquid. Add to the wok with the black beans and stir until thickened. Return the mussels to the pan and heat through, stirring. Season and serve immediately.

ASPARAGUS IN PROSCIUTTO

SERVES 4

This dish also works well served as 'finger food' for a party or buffet. Use fairly thick asparagus spears – they are easier to wrap.

12 asparagus spears, trimmed
90 ml (3 fl oz) quality olive oil
2 tablespoons white wine vinegar
1 teaspoon wholegrain mustard
salt and pepper to taste
12 thin slices prosciutto

1 Place the asparagus in a large pan of boiling salted water and cook for about 8 minutes until tender. Drain, then plunge the asparagus spears into cold water to preserve the colour.

2 Mix together the olive oil, vinegar, mustard and seasoning in a shallow dish.

3 Drain the asparagus thoroughly and toss in the olive oil mixture until well coated.

4 Carefully wrap each asparagus spear in a slice of prosciutto.

5 Arrange the asparagus spears on a serving platter and serve with crusty Italian bread.

MARINATED BABY AUBERGINES

SERVES 4

If baby aubergines are unavailable use the larger variety, cut into quarters. The flavour of this dish is even better if it is made the day before.

12 baby aubergines, halved lengthwise
225 ml (8 fl oz) quality olive oil
juice of 1 lemon
2 tablespoons red wine vinegar
3 cloves
3 tablespoons pine nuts
3 tablespoons sultanas
1 tablespoon sugar
1 bay leaf
large pinch of dried crushed chillies
salt and pepper to taste
rocket leaves to garnish

1 Preheat grill to medium high. Brush the aubergines with olive oil and place, cut side up, in the grill pan. Grill for 10 minutes, until slightly blackened, turning halfway through cooking.

2 Mix together the remaining olive oil, lemon juice, vinegar, cloves, pine nuts, sultanas, sugar, bay leaf, chillies and seasoning.

3 Place the hot aubergines in a shallow dish and pour over the marinade. Leave to cool, turning occasionally.

4 Serve cold, garnished with rocket leaves.

ARTICHOKE WITH GOAT'S CHEESE

SERVES 6

Canned artichoke bottoms make this dish a sophisticated starter that can be assembled in minutes. Look out for olive purée in good delicatessens. Alternatively, use finely chopped black olives.

2×297 g (10 oz) cans artichoke bottoms
4 tablespoons olive purée
2 crottins (small, round goat's cheese)
25 g (1 oz) flaked almonds

TO SERVE
salad leaves, eg radicchio, frisée and lamb's
   lettuce
olive oil for drizzling

1 Preheat grill to medium. Drain the artichoke bottoms, rinse and dry thoroughly on kitchen paper. Trim the bases if necessary to enable them to stand upright.

2 Divide the olive purée between the artichokes, spreading it into the hollows.

3 Cut the crottins into the same number of slices as there are artichoke bottoms. Place a crottin slice on each artichoke and sprinkle with almonds.

4 Grill for 5-10 minutes, until the cheese is melting and the almonds are browned.

5 Divide the salad leaves between individual serving plates. Place the artichoke bottoms on the plates and drizzle with a little olive oil. Serve immediately.

STUFFED MUSHROOMS

SERVES 4

Try using walnuts or almonds instead of the hazelnuts in this tasty filling.

12 even-sized open cup mushrooms
1 tablespoon olive oil
15 g (½ oz) butter
½ small onion, chopped
2 tablespoons chopped hazelnuts
1 clove garlic, crushed
150 g (5 oz) frozen chopped spinach, defrosted
   and squeezed dry
25 g (1 oz) feta cheese, crumbled
25 g (1 oz) Cheddar cheese, crumbled
1 tablespoon dried dill
salt and pepper to taste
dill sprigs and salad leaves to garnish

1 Preheat oven to 200°C (400°F/Gas 6).

2 Remove the stems from the mushrooms and chop them roughly.

3 Heat the olive oil and butter in a pan, add the onion and cook until soft. Add the chopped mushroom stems, nuts and garlic and cook for 1 minute. Add the spinach and cook for 5 minutes, stirring. Remove from the heat and stir in the cheeses and dill.

4 Arrange the mushrooms cup side up in a baking dish. Season the stuffing and divide equally between them.

5 Bake for 10 minutes or until the filling is lightly browned. Serve immediately, garnished with dill and salad leaves.

TURKEY & BACON KEBABS

SERVES 4

I prefer to use smoked bacon to wrap round the turkey. I also like to cook these kebabs until the bacon is really crisp.

6 rashers smoked streaky bacon, derinded
75 g (3 oz) boneless turkey, cubed

SAUCE
75 g (3 oz) fromage frais
2 teaspoons horseradish sauce
2 teaspoons coarse grain (Meaux) mustard
salt and pepper to taste

TO GARNISH
salad leaves

1. Stretch the bacon with the back of a knife, then cut each rasher into 3 pieces.

2. Wrap each piece of bacon round a cube of turkey and thread on to 4 skewers.

3. To make the sauce, mix the fromage frais with the horseradish, mustard and seasoning.

4. Preheat the grill to medium. Put the kebabs on a rack in a grill pan and grill for 8-10 minutes, turning once, until the bacon is crisp.

5. Serve immediately, garnished with salad leaves, and accompanied by the sauce.

HONEY GLAZED CHICKEN WINGS

SERVES 4

A starter with a Chinese flavour, which can be cooked on a barbecue. As these tasty chicken wings are best eaten with your fingers, make sure you have plenty of napkins to hand.

8 chicken wings

GLAZE
2 tablespoons clear honey
1 tablespoon tomato sauce
2 tablespoons hoisin sauce

PEKING CUCUMBER
1/2 cucumber, peeled and sliced
2 tablespoons rice wine or cider vinegar
1 teaspoon soy sauce
1/2 teaspoon salt

TO GARNISH
shredded spring onion

1. For the glaze, mix together the honey, tomato and hoisin sauces in a bowl. Brush over the chicken wings to coat completely.

2. To prepare the Peking Cucumber, cut the cucumber slices into quarters and place in a bowl with the vinegar, soy sauce and salt. Stir well, then leave to stand for 15 minutes, stirring occasionally.

3. Preheat the grill to medium. Put the chicken wings on a rack in the grill pan and grill for 8-10 minutes until well cooked and dark brown, turning once. Serve immediately, garnished with spring onion and accompanied by the Peking Cucumber.

ABOVE: HONEY GLAZED CHICKEN WINGS *BELOW*: TURKEY & BACON KEBABS

VEGETABLE TEMPURA

SERVES 4

The variety of vegetables you can use for this Japanese dish is endless.

1 red pepper, cored, seeded and cut into thick strips
1 courgette, in 1 cm (½ inch) slices
8 shitake or oyster mushrooms
50 g (2 oz) mangetout, trimmed
1 sweet potato, in 5 mm (¼ inch) slices
8 baby corn cobs
vegetable oil for deep-frying

BATTER
150 g (5 oz) plain flour
1 teaspoon baking powder
1 egg yolk
350 ml (12 fl oz) ice cold water

DIPPING SAUCE
3 tablespoons mirin (or medium sherry)
3 tablespoons light soy sauce
225 ml (8 fl oz) chicken stock
½ teaspoon chopped fresh root ginger

1 To make the batter, sift the flour and baking powder into a bowl. Mix the egg yolk with the water, then gradually add to the flour mixture, beating until smooth.

2 To make the sauce, gently heat the ingredients together in a pan; keep warm.

3 Half-fill a wok or deep pan with oil, and heat to 190°C (375°F). Dip the vegetables, a few at a time, into the batter and fry in the oil until lightly golden, about 1 minute. Drain on kitchen paper.

4 Serve the vegetable tempura immediately, with the dipping sauce.

SPICY GLASS NOODLE SALAD

SERVES 4

Cellophane noodles, also called glass noodles, are made from mung beans. Like dried cloud ear mushrooms, they are available from Oriental stores. You can use sliced button mushrooms instead of cloud ears if you prefer.

2 cloves garlic, crushed
1 tablespoon light soy sauce
4 tablespoons sugar
1 red chilli, seeded and finely sliced
1 tablespoon sesame oil
pepper to taste
150 g (5 oz) frozen prawns, defrosted
50 g (2 oz) cellophane noodles
1 carrot, cut into fine strips
1 courgette, cut into fine strips
5 dried cloud ear mushrooms, soaked in hot water until soft (optional)
1 tablespoon toasted sesame seeds

1 Mix together the garlic, soy sauce, sugar, chilli, sesame oil and pepper in a bowl. Add the prawns and toss well.

2 Cut the noodles into 10 cm (4 inch) lengths. Cook the noodles and carrot in boiling water for 1 minute. Add the courgette and cook for 1 minute. Drain and refresh in cold water. Drain thoroughly.

3 Place all the ingredients in a bowl and toss well to combine before serving.

ABOVE: VEGETABLE TEMPURA BELOW: SPICY GLASS NOODLE SALAD

POTATO SKINS WITH HERB DIP

SERVES 4

Use a floury variety of potatoes, such as King Edwards. Cook the potatoes in the microwave for extra speed – allowing 10-12 minutes on high per 500 g (1 lb), turning occasionally.

4 medium baking potatoes
sunflower oil for brushing
salt and pepper to taste

DIP
125 ml (4 fl oz) low-fat fromage frais
2 tablespoons chopped chives
1 tablespoon chopped parsley

TO GARNISH
snipped chives

1 Preheat oven to 220°C (425°F/Gas 7).

2 Cook the potatoes in boiling salted water for 10-15 minutes until almost tender. Drain and cool.

3 Cut the potatoes into quarters and gently scrape out most of the flesh, leaving a 1 cm (½ inch) layer. Cut in half again.

4 Place the potato 'skins' on a baking tray, brush with a little oil and sprinkle with salt and pepper. Bake for 15-20 minutes until golden.

5 For the dip, mix together the fromage frais, chives and parsley in a small bowl. Season with salt and pepper. Sprinkle with chives.

6 Serve the hot potato skins with the herb dip.

GUACAMOLE

SERVES 4-6

Fresh coriander makes this Mexican avocado dip truly authentic. Served with corn chips or crudités, it makes a good party dish. Use tabasco if fresh chillies are unavailable.

2 large ripe avocados, peeled and chopped
1 small onion, chopped
3 ripe tomatoes, chopped
juice of 1 lime
1 green chilli, seeded and chopped
1 tablespoon chopped coriander leaves
salt and pepper to taste

TO SERVE
coriander sprigs
chilli slices
corn chips

1 Place the avocados, onion, tomatoes, lime juice, chilli and coriander in a food processor or blender and work to a rough purée.

2 Season with salt and pepper.

3 Transfer to a serving bowl and garnish with coriander and chilli. Serve the guacamole with corn chips.

ABOVE: POTATO SKINS WITH HERB DIP *BELOW*: GUACAMOLE

MEXICAN TOMATO SALAD

SERVES 4-6

The dressing for this salad can be made up to a day in advance, as the flavours improve with keeping. Do not mix until just before serving, otherwise the pasta will soften as it absorbs the dressing on standing.

250 g (8 oz) tricolour pasta spirals
¼ Spanish onion, chopped
250 g (8 oz) ripe tomatoes, chopped
½ green chilli, seeded and chopped
3 tablespoons chopped coriander leaves
juice of 2 limes
4 sun-dried tomatoes
salt and pepper to taste
coriander leaves to garnish

1 Bring a large saucepan of salted water to the boil. Add the pasta, stir once and boil for 10-12 minutes until tender. Drain, then refresh under cold water. Drain well and toss in a little oil to prevent sticking.

2 Place the onion, tomatoes, chilli, coriander and lime juice in a food processor and blend until fairly smooth. Add one of the sun-dried tomatoes, with salt and pepper, and blend again briefly.

3 Just before serving toss the pasta in the dressing. Slice the remaining sun-dried tomatoes and sprinkle over the salad. Garnish with coriander leaves to serve.

PEPERONATA PASTA SALAD

SERVES 4-6

I love the sweet, slightly charred taste of grilled peppers. Serve this as a starter or accompaniment to grilled food.

280 g (8 oz) chiocciole or pasta spirals
1 red pepper
1 yellow pepper
1 green pepper
2 tablespoons chopped spring onions

DRESSING
250 g (8 oz) tomatoes, skinned, seeded and
  chopped
2 tablespoons olive oil
1 tablespoon lemon juice
2 cloves garlic, chopped
1 teaspoon paprika
salt and pepper to taste

1 Bring a large saucepan of salted water to the boil. Add the pasta, stir once and boil for 10-12 minutes until tender. Drain, then refresh under cold water and drain thoroughly. Toss in a little oil to prevent sticking.

2 Preheat the grill to high and grill the peppers, turning occasionally, until their skins are charred. When cool enough to handle, peel off the skins. Halve the peppers, discard seeds and cut the flesh into thin strips. Place in a large bowl, with the pasta and spring onions. Mix lightly.

3 Place all the dressing ingredients in a food processor or blender and work until fairly smooth. Pour over the salad and toss lightly to serve.

CHICKEN LIVERS WITH SALAD LEAVES

SERVES 3-4

This quantity is sufficient to serve four as a starter or three as a light main course accompanied by crusty bread or toast.

---

about 250 g (8 oz) mixed salad leaves, e.g. frisée
   (curly endive), chicory and lamb's lettuce
25 g (1 oz) unsalted butter
3 tablespoons olive or groundnut oil
500 g (1 lb) chicken livers, halved
1 small red onion, quartered and separated into
   petals
1 tablespoon red wine vinegar
1 teaspoon Dijon mustard
4 tablespoons brandy
1 teaspoon chopped thyme
salt and pepper to taste

TO GARNISH
thyme sprigs

1 Arrange the mixed salad leaves on individual serving plates.

2 Heat the butter and oil in a large frying pan or wok. Add the chicken livers and stir fry over a high heat for 2 minutes to seal. Add the onion and continue stir frying for 2 minutes until the chicken livers are browned on the outside but still pink and tender within.

3 Add the vinegar, mustard, brandy and thyme and toss gently over the heat to mix. Add seasoning.

4 Spoon the chicken mixture and juices on top of the salad leaves and serve at once, garnished with thyme sprigs.

BACON WRAPPED PRAWN SALAD

SERVES 4

This is a wonderful summer lunch. I also make a simplified version – omitting the cooked vegetables – to serve as a starter.

½ head oakleaf lettuce
about 75 g (3 oz) rocket
175 g (6 oz) red or yellow cherry tomatoes,
   halved
6 rashers streaky bacon, rinds removed
12 cooked King prawns, peeled and deveined
3 tablespoons olive oil
250 g (8 oz) mangetout
½ red or yellow pepper, cored, seeded and cut
   into thin strips
2 tablespoons walnut or hazelnut oil
2 tablespoons tarragon or wine vinegar
grated rind and juice of ½ lemon
pepper to taste

1 Tear the salad leaves into bite-sized pieces and arrange on individual serving plates with the cherry tomatoes.

2 Cut each bacon rasher in half and stretch, using the back of a knife. Wrap a half rasher around each prawn.

3 Heat the olive oil in a wok or large frying pan. Add the bacon-wrapped prawns and stir fry over a fairly high heat for 3 minutes. Add the mangetout and pepper strips and stir fry for 2 minutes.

4 Add the nut oil, vinegar, lemon rind and juice. Toss gently and season with pepper. Spoon over the salad and serve at once.

ABOVE: CHICKEN LIVERS WITH SALAD LEAVES *BELOW*: BACON-WRAPPED PRAWN SALAD

GADO GADO

SERVES 4-6

A protein-packed Indonesian salad, combining crisply cooked and raw vegetables, ribbons of omelette and a spicy peanut sauce. Vary the vegetables as you like – to include baby corn cobs, leeks, French beans or cauliflower if you prefer.

2 eggs
3 tablespoons groundnut oil
250 g (8 oz) carrot
3 celery sticks
1 clove garlic, halved
125 g (4 oz) mangetout
½ head Chinese leaf, shredded
175 g (6 oz) bean sprouts
125 g (4 oz) radishes, sliced

PEANUT SAUCE
25 g (1 oz) creamed coconut
6 tablespoons milk
¼ onion, chopped
1 clove garlic, crushed
4 tablespoons peanut butter
½ teaspoon ground cumin
½ teaspoon chilli powder
1 tablespoon soy sauce
pinch of sugar

1 First make the peanut sauce: chop the creamed coconut and place in a blender or food processor with the milk. Blend to a paste. Add all the remaining ingredients and purée until smooth.

2 To prepare the omelette, lightly beat the eggs with 2 tablespoons water. Heat 1 tablespoon of the oil in a large non-stick frying pan and add the beaten egg. Cook over a medium heat using a spatula to push the cooked edges into the centre and tilting the pan as the omelette cooks. When the omelette is golden brown underneath, turn to cook the underside. Remove from the pan and set aside.

3 Cut the carrot and celery into julienne (matchstick strips). Heat the remaining oil in the same pan or wok. Add the garlic, carrot, celery and mangetout and stir fry for 2-3 minutes until just tender. Transfer to a salad bowl, discarding the garlic, and allow to cool.

4 Cut the prepared omelette into thin ribbons and add to the salad bowl with the Chinese leaf, bean sprouts and radishes. Toss gently to mix.

5 Spoon the peanut sauce over the salad to serve.

Note This looks most attractive garnished with radish roses. Simply make crosswise cuts through the radish from the top almost through to the base and leave in a bowl of iced water for about 20 minutes to open out.

MANGO, CHICKEN & SPINACH SALAD

SERVES 4

Serve this delicious combination as a substantial starter or light meal.

1 large ripe mango
3 skinless chicken breast fillets
175 g (6 oz) young spinach leaves
1 teaspoon sesame oil
5 tablespoons groundnut or olive oil
1 clove garlic, crushed
3 spring onions, sliced
2 tablespoons sherry vinegar
½ teaspoon soft dark brown sugar
50 g (2 oz) salted cashew nuts
handful of coriander leaves
salt and pepper to taste

1 Peel the mango and slice thinly, discarding the stone. Cut the chicken crosswise into strips.

2 Tear the spinach into bite-size pieces and arrange on individual plates.

3 Heat the sesame oil and 3 tablespoons groundnut or olive oil in a wok. Add the chicken and stir fry over a high heat for 2 minutes. Add the garlic and continue stir frying for 1 minute. Stir in the spring onions and cook for a few seconds.

4 Add the remaining oil to the wok with the vinegar and sugar. Stir in the mango, cashews, coriander and seasoning; heat through.

5 Spoon the chicken mixture on top of the spinach leaves and serve at once.

CHEESE SALAD WITH MIXED HOT NUTS

SERVES 4

A lightly dressed salad with garlic and herb cheese and hot, spicy nuts. Use other kinds of nuts if you prefer, such as walnuts, pecans and hazelnuts.

1 head lollo rosso, roughly torn
50 g (2 oz) rocket
handful of chervil sprigs, roughly torn
2 celery sticks, chopped
1 red apple, cored and sliced
142 g (5 oz) Boursin with garlic and herbs

DRESSING
2 tablespoons olive oil
1 tablespoon red wine vinegar
pinch of sugar
salt and pepper to taste

MIXED NUTS
50 g (2 oz) blanched almonds
50 g (2 oz) peanuts or cashews
25 g (1 oz) pine nuts
25 g (1 oz) butter
½ teaspoon paprika
½ teaspoon mild chilli powder
pinch of ground cumin
sea salt to taste

1 Put the salad leaves and chervil in a bowl with the celery and apple.

2 Mix together the dressing ingredients, add to the salad and toss gently to coat. Crumble the soft cheese over the top.

3 Stir fry the nuts in a frying pan over medium heat for 4-5 minutes to brown. Add the butter and stir fry for 1 minute until sizzling. Stir in the spices and salt. Let cool for 1 minute. Sprinkle over salad and serve.

ABOVE: MANGO, CHICKEN & SPINACH SALAD *BELOW*: CHEESE SALAD WITH MIXED HOT NUTS

PASTA, WATERCRESS & CASHEW NUT SALAD

SERVES 4-6

This simple fresh-tasting salad is delicious served with cold meats, or barbecued food.

175 g (6 oz) pasta shells
1 bunch of watercress
125 g (4 oz) cashew nuts
1 red pepper, cored, seeded and diced

DRESSING
2 tablespoons walnut oil
1 tablespoon wine vinegar
2 teaspoons Dijon mustard
1 tablespoon snipped chives
salt and pepper to taste

1. Bring a large saucepan of salted water to the boil. Add the pasta shells, stir once and boil for 10-12 minutes until tender. Drain, then refresh under cold water and drain thoroughly. Toss in a little oil to prevent sticking.

2. Place the pasta in a serving bowl. Roughly chop the watercress, then add to the pasta with the nuts and red pepper; mix lightly.

3. Place all the dressing ingredients in a small bowl and whisk together with a fork. Pour over the salad and toss lightly just before serving.

TRICOLORE SALAD

SERVES 4-6

Capture all the flavours of summer with this colourful salad. Use *amori* (pasta knots) or spirals.

250 g (8 oz) pasta knots or spirals
1 ripe avocado
lemon juice for sprinkling
250 g (8 oz) cherry tomatoes, quartered
125 g (4 oz) mozzarella cheese, diced
handful of basil leaves, shredded if large

DRESSING
1 tablespoon mayonnaise
2 tablespoons olive oil
1 tablespoon wine vinegar
1 teaspoon sugar
1 clove garlic, crushed
salt and pepper to taste

1. Bring a large saucepan of salted water to the boil. Add the pasta, stir once and boil for 10-12 minutes until tender. Drain, then refresh under cold water and drain thoroughly. Toss in a little oil to prevent sticking.

2. Place the pasta in a bowl. Peel, stone and dice the avocado. Toss in a little lemon juice to prevent discoloration. Add to the pasta with the tomatoes, mozzarella and basil.

3. Place the dressing ingredients in a small bowl and whisk together with a fork. Pour over the salad, toss lightly and serve immediately.

ARTICHOKE & CHICKEN SALAD

SERVES 4

Use quality black olives in this salad as their flavour is quite dominant. Canned artichokes in brine can be used in place of artichokes in oil, but the latter have a better flavour. Serve this tasty salad with plenty of crusty bread.

350 g (12 oz) cooked chicken
6 tomatoes, skinned and cut into wedges
50 g (2 oz) black olives, halved and stoned
275 g (9 oz) bottled artichokes in oil, drained
   and quartered
2 tablespoons chopped basil

CAPER DRESSING
4 tablespoons olive oil
2 tablespoons wine vinegar
2 cloves garlic, crushed
1 tablespoon coarse grain (Meaux) mustard
½ teaspoon clear honey
1 tablespoon chopped capers
salt and pepper to taste

TO GARNISH
curly endive (frisée)

1 To make the dressing, put all the ingredients in a screw-topped jar and shake together thoroughly until blended.

2 Cut the chicken into pieces, put into a bowl, pour over the dressing and leave to marinate for 10 minutes.

3 Add the tomatoes, olives, artichokes and basil. Toss well to mix and turn into a serving dish. Garnish with curly endive.

TURKEY TONNATO

SERVES 4

Slices of turkey coated in a tuna fish sauce – an adaptation of an Italian recipe that features veal.

500 g (1 lb) cooked turkey
4 curled radicchio leaves

TUNA FISH SAUCE
75 g (3 oz) can tuna fish, drained
125 g (4 oz) fromage frais
1 tablespoon anchovy essence
1 tablespoon lemon juice
salt and pepper to taste
4 tablespoons mayonnaise
a little milk (optional)

TO GARNISH
1 tablespoon capers
lemon slices
herb sprigs

1 To make the sauce, put the tuna fish and fromage frais in a food processor or blender with the anchovy essence, lemon juice and seasoning. Blend until the mixture is smooth. Fold into the mayonnaise, adding a little milk if the mixture becomes too stiff.

2 Cut the turkey into finger sized pieces and mix with half of the tuna sauce.

3 Place a curled radicchio leaf on each serving plate. Spoon some turkey mixture into each leaf and spoon the remaining tuna sauce over the top. Garnish with capers, lemon slices and herbs to serve.

SALADE TIÈDE

SERVES 4

This is one of my favourite summer salads, and it is so quick to prepare. Have all the salad leaves ready and simply fry the bacon and chicken livers just before you're ready to eat.

1 oak leaf lettuce
½ curly endive (frisée)
few radicchio leaves
few rocket leaves
2 heads chicory, diagonally sliced
3 tablespoons olive oil
2 cloves garlic, sliced
125 g (4 oz) smoked streaky bacon, derinded and
  cut into strips
250 g (8 oz) chicken livers
3 tablespoons cider vinegar
salt and pepper to taste
50 g (2 oz) chopped walnuts

1 Tear the lettuce, endive and radicchio into manageable sized pieces and put into a salad bowl with the rocket leaves and chicory.

2 Heat the oil in a frying pan, add the garlic, bacon and chicken livers and fry for 5-6 minutes until tender but still pink inside, stirring occasionally.

3 Slice the chicken livers and scatter over the salad with the bacon.

4 Pour the vinegar into the pan and stir round to mix with the liver juices. Add seasoning, then pour over the salad. Sprinkle the chopped walnuts on top to serve.

CHICKEN & BROCCOLI SALAD

SERVES 4

You can use any blue cheese for this dressing. Stilton makes an excellent alternative.

125 g (4 oz) cauliflower
250 g (8 oz) broccoli
350 g (12 oz) cooked chicken, cut into strips
125 g (4 oz) streaky bacon, derinded and
  chopped

ROQUEFORT DRESSING
50 g (2 oz) Roquefort
150 ml (¼ pint) single cream
2 tablespoons chopped chives
salt and pepper to taste

1 Break the cauliflower and broccoli into small florets and cook in boiling salted water for 4 minutes. Drain thoroughly and put into a bowl with the chicken.

2 Fry the bacon in its own fat until crisp; drain and set aside.

3 To make the dressing, mash the cheese with a fork and gradually mix in the cream to form a smooth paste. Stir in the chives and seasoning.

4 Pour the dressing over the salad and toss well to coat completely. Turn into a shallow serving dish and sprinkle with the bacon to serve.

HOT BACON & PECAN SALAD

SERVES 4

Chicory is one of my favourite 'hot' salad ingredients. The firm texture is retained, while its bitter flavour is pleasantly tempered by the heat of the dressing.

2 heads chicory
½ head frisée (curly endive)
1 bunch watercress
1 orange, peeled and segmented
½ onion, thinly sliced
4 tablespoons olive oil
250 g (8 oz) bacon rashers, derinded and chopped
1 clove garlic, crushed
50 g (2 oz) pecans
3 tablespoons freshly squeezed orange juice
2 tablespoons sherry vinegar
1 teaspoon Dijon mustard
salt and pepper to taste

1 Arrange the chicory, frisée (endive), watercress, orange and onion on individual plates.

2 Heat 2 tablespoons oil in a large frying pan or wok. Add the bacon and stir fry for 2 minutes. Stir in the garlic and pecans and cook for 1 minute.

3 Add the remaining oil to the pan together with the orange juice, vinegar, mustard and seasoning. Stir well.

4 Spoon the hot dressing over the salad and serve at once.

SALAMI & OMELETTE SALAD

SERVES 4

2 eggs
15 g (½ oz) butter
1 cos lettuce, roughly torn
75 g (3 oz) salami, finely sliced
handful of black olives
4 tablespoons olive oil
½ red pepper, cored, seeded and cut into thin strips
2 tablespoons capers
2 tablespoons wine vinegar
½ teaspoon Dijon mustard
pinch of sugar
salt and pepper to taste

1 Lightly beat the eggs with 2 tablespoons water. Melt the butter in a large non-stick frying pan and add the beaten egg. Cook over a medium heat, using a spatula to push the cooked edges into the centre and tilting the pan, until the omelette is softly set. Transfer to a plate, roll up and allow to cool. Slice the omelette and arrange on a serving plate with the lettuce, salami and olives.

2 Add the olive oil to the pan and return to the heat. Add the pepper strips and stir fry for 1 minute. Stir in the remaining ingredients.

3 Spoon the hot dressing over the salad to serve.

SPAGHETTI WITH TUNA & ANCHOVY

SERVES 4

This tuna and anchovy sauce – bursting with flavour – is just the thing to rustle up in a few minutes when you're in a hurry.

250g (8 oz) spaghetti
3 tablespoons olive oil
2 cloves garlic, chopped
½ chilli, seeded and chopped
25 g (1 oz) parsley, finely chopped
4 anchovy fillets, chopped
192 g (7 oz) can tuna in oil
salt and pepper to taste
parsley sprigs to garnish

1 Bring a large pan of salted water to the boil. Add the pasta, stir once and boil for 10-12 minutes until tender.

2 Meanwhile make the sauce. Heat the oil in a frying pan, add the garlic, chilli and parsley and fry gently, stirring, for 2 minutes. Add the anchovies and stir well until they start to dissolve.

3 Flake the tuna with its oil and add to the pan, stirring well. Season with pepper, and salt if necessary. Drain the pasta and mix together with the sauce. Serve immediately, garnished with parsley.

SPAGHETTI WITH CLAMS & LEEKS

SERVES 4

Keep a can of clams in your cupboard and you can put together this sauce in no time. When time is less pressing, use freshly cooked, shelled clams or mussels.

250 g (8 oz) spaghetti
25 g (1 oz) butter
2 leeks, thinly sliced
150 ml (¼ pint) dry white wine
pinch of powdered saffron
250 g (8 oz) can clams, drained
1 tablespoon chopped parsley
3 tablespoons double cream
salt and pepper to taste
parsley sprigs to garnish

1 Bring a large pan of salted water to the boil. Add the pasta, stir once and boil for 10-12 minutes until tender.

2 Meanwhile make the sauce. Melt the butter in a small pan, add the leeks and fry gently for about 5 minutes, until softened. Add the wine and saffron, bring to the boil, then boil steadily for about 5 minutes, until reduced by half.

3 Stir in the clams, parsley, cream, salt and pepper, then heat through gently.

4 Drain the spaghetti and toss with the sauce. Serve garnished with parsley.

PRAWN KORMA

SERVES 4

Prawns don't need a lengthy cooking time so stir frying is the perfect way to cook this mild Indian curry. Buy creamed coconut in blocks from supermarkets or ethnic stores.

25 g (1 oz) butter
2 tablespoons oil
2 onions, cut into wedges
250 g (8 oz) potato, diced
1-2 cloves garlic, crushed
2.5 cm (1 inch) piece fresh root ginger, grated
1 chilli, seeded and chopped
2 teaspoons ground coriander
1 teaspoon ground cumin
1½ teaspoons turmeric
½ teaspoon allspice
25 g (1 oz) creamed coconut, chopped
300 ml (½ pint) light stock or water
12 cooked King prawns
75 g (3 oz) frozen peas, thawed
1 tablespoon roughly chopped coriander leaves
2 tablespoons cream or thick yogurt

TO GARNISH
coriander leaves

1 Heat the butter and oil in a large shallow pan or wok. Add the onions, potato and garlic and stir fry for 5 minutes to soften. Stir in the ginger, chilli and spices and fry gently for a further 4 minutes.

2 Add the creamed coconut and stock or water to the pan. Bring to the boil and simmer for 5 minutes. Stir in the prawns, peas and coriander. Cover and cook for 2-3 minutes.

3 Stir in the cream or yogurt and seasoning. Serve hot, garnished with coriander and accompanied by basmati rice.

MONKFISH WITH OKRA & TOMATO

SERVES 4

625 g (1¼ lb) monkfish fillet
250 g (8 oz) okra
4 tablespoons wine vinegar
3 tablespoons virgin olive oil
3 rashers smoked bacon, derinded and chopped
1 onion, chopped
1-2 cloves garlic, crushed
500 g (1 lb) tomatoes, skinned and cut into
   wedges
3 basil sprigs
1 thyme sprig
200 ml (7 fl oz) dry white wine
2 tablespoons chopped parsley
salt and pepper to taste

TO GARNISH
herb sprigs

1 Cut the fish into 2.5 cm (1 inch) slices.

2 Cut the okra diagonally into thick slices. Place in a bowl and add water to cover. Add the vinegar and leave to stand for 10 minutes then rinse thoroughly and pat dry.

3 Heat the oil in a wok or large sauté pan with a lid. Add the bacon, onion and garlic and stir fry over a medium heat for 3 minutes to soften. Stir in the tomatoes, basil, thyme and wine and cook for 2 minutes.

4 Add the okra and monkfish to the pan, together with the parsley and seasoning. Cover and cook for about 4 minutes until the monkfish is firm and opaque and the okra is just tender. Serve immediately, garnished with herbs.

STIR FRIED FISH WITH TOMATO & HERBS

SERVES 4

Choose firm white fish for this recipe, such as cod, haddock or monkfish, and select herbs according to preference. Serve with plain boiled rice.

3 tablespoons virgin olive oil
1 clove garlic, crushed
2 celery sticks, cut into julienne strips
3 spring onions, diagonally sliced
125 ml (4 fl oz) dry white wine
2 teaspoons tomato purée
pinch of sugar
500 g (1 lb) white fish fillet, skinned and cut into
  chunks
125 g (4 oz) mangetout
3 tomatoes, skinned and cut into wedges
2 tablespoons chopped herbs, e.g. coriander, basil,
  parsley, chives
salt and pepper to taste

TO GARNISH
herb sprigs

1. Heat the oil in a large frying pan or wok. Add the garlic, celery and spring onions and stir fry for 1 minute. Stir in the dry white wine, tomato purée and sugar.

2. Add the fish to the pan, cover and cook for 2-3 minutes.

3. Gently stir in the mangetout, tomatoes and herbs. Cook for 1-2 minutes until the fish is firm and the mangetout are just tender. Season and serve garnished with herb sprigs.

SCALLOPS IN SAFFRON CREAM SAUCE

SERVES 4

Succulent plump scallops are stir fried with celery and carrot and served in a wine and cream sauce flavoured with saffron. Serve with rice – preferably a mixture of white and wild rice.

pinch of saffron threads
25 g (1 oz) butter
1 shallot, finely chopped
3 celery sticks, cut into julienne strips
2 carrots, cut into julienne strips
12 large scallops
125 ml (4 fl oz) dry white wine
4 tablespoons double cream
salt and pepper to taste

TO GARNISH
chervil

1. Place the saffron threads in a cup and add 125 ml (4 fl oz) boiling water. Leave to infuse for 15 minutes.

2. Heat the butter in a large frying pan or wok. Add the shallot, celery and carrots and stir fry for 1 minute. Add the scallops and stir fry for 1 minute.

3. Stir in the wine and saffron with its liquid. Bring to the boil, cover and allow to simmer for 4-5 minutes until the scallops are just firm and cooked. Stir in the cream and seasoning and heat through gently.

4. Serve immediately, sprinkled with chervil.

COD WITH BROCCOLI & RED PEPPER

SERVES 3-4

Quick fried pieces of cod with broccoli, red onion and pepper in black bean sauce. Use canned rather than dried beans and rinse well as they are salty.

1 egg white
4 teaspoons cornflour
2 tablespoons soy sauce
500 g (1 lb) cod fillet, skinned and cubed
150 ml (¼ pint) groundnut oil
1 clove garlic, crushed
2.5 cm (1 inch) piece fresh root ginger, grated
1 small red onion, cut into wedges
175 g (6 oz) broccoli florets
1 red pepper, cored, seeded and cut into strips
3 tablespoons sherry
2 tablespoons oyster sauce
2 tablespoons canned black beans, rinsed
pepper to taste

1. Whisk the egg white until frothy and stir in 3 teaspoons cornflour and 1 tablespoon soy sauce. Add the fish and mix well.

2. Heat the oil in a wok. Fry the fish, in batches, for about 2 minutes until cooked through. Drain on kitchen paper; set aside.

3. Pour off all but 3 tablespoons oil from the wok. Add the garlic, ginger, onion, broccoli and red pepper and stir fry for 3 minutes.

4. Mix together the remaining cornflour, soy sauce, sherry, oyster sauce and 2 tablespoons water. Add to the wok with the black beans and pepper; stir until thickened.

5. Return the fish to the wok and heat through, stirring gently. Serve at once.

SWEET & SOUR FISH BALLS

SERVES 4

Serve this tasty stir fry with simple egg fried rice, or herb and sesame noodles.

3 tablespoons groundnut oil
1 clove garlic, crushed
125 g (4 oz) mangetout
1 carrot, diagonally sliced
125 g (4 oz) baby corn cobs, halved lengthwise
2 spring onions, sliced
227 g (8 oz) can pineapple pieces in juice
125 ml (4 fl oz) chicken or fish stock
2 tablespoons sherry
3 tablespoons wine vinegar
2 tablespoons light soy sauce
1 tablespoon cornflour
1 tablespoon sugar

FISH BALLS
350 g (12 oz) cod fillet, skinned and diced
125 g (4 oz) peeled prawns
2 spring onions, chopped
1 tablespoon sherry
1 tablespoon light soy sauce
1 egg white
salt and pepper to taste

1. Put all the ingredients for the fish balls in a food processor or blender and process until almost smooth. With dampened hands, shape the mixture into 16 balls.

2. Heat the oil in a wok. Add the garlic and vegetables and stir fry for 2 minutes. Add the pineapple, reserving the juice.

3. Blend the pineapple juice with the remaining ingredients and add to the wok. Stir until thickened. Add the fish balls, cover and cook gently for 4-5 minutes until the fish is opaque and cooked.

SIZZLING TROUT WITH GARLIC & SPRING ONIONS

SERVES 2

For a fast lunch or supper try this simply delicious pan-fried trout with garlic, spring onions, parsley and a hint of ginger and lemon. Serve with new potatoes and a salad.

2 trout, cleaned
25 g (1 oz) butter
2 tablespoons virgin olive oil
2 cloves garlic, thinly sliced
½ teaspoon grated fresh root ginger
4 spring onions, sliced
1 tablespoon chopped parsley
juice of ½ lemon
¼ teaspoon finely grated lemon rind
salt and pepper to taste

TO GARNISH
lemon wedges

1 Wash the trout and remove the heads. Using a sharp knife, make 2 or 3 slashes through the skin on each side of the fish.

2 Heat 15 g (½ oz) of the butter and 1 tablespoon oil in a large frying pan. Add the trout and fry for about 4 minutes on each side until just cooked. Transfer to a plate and keep hot.

3 Add the rest of the butter and oil to the pan. Add the garlic, ginger and spring onions and stir fry for 1 minute, then stir in the remaining ingredients and return the trout to the pan. Cook for 1 minute over a high heat until hot and sizzling. Serve at once, garnished with lemon wedges.

SMOKED HADDOCK WITH SPRING VEGETABLES

SERVES 4

Serve this tasty dish of smoked haddock, young carrots and courgettes in a herb and cream sauce with rice or pasta.

25 g (1 oz) butter
250 g (8 oz) small baby carrots, halved lengthwise
2 small courgettes, cut into julienne strips
4 spring onions, cut into 5 cm (2 inch) lengths
juice of ½ lemon
500 g (1 lb) smoked haddock fillet, skinned and diced
300 ml (½ pint) milk
1 teaspoon chopped parsley
1 teaspoon chopped tarragon
4 tablespoons double cream
pepper to taste

TO GARNISH
tarragon sprigs

1 Heat the butter in a large shallow pan or wok. Add the vegetables and stir fry for 2 minutes. Add the lemon juice and smoked haddock and stir fry for 2 minutes, taking care not to break up the fish.

2 Add the milk to the pan and bring to the boil. Lower the heat and simmer for 4-5 minutes until the fish is cooked.

3 Gently stir in the parsley, tarragon, cream and seasoning. Serve, garnished with tarragon.

ABOVE: SIZZLING TROUT WITH GARLIC & SPRING ONIONS *BELOW:* SMOKED HADDOCK WITH SPRING VEGETABLES

PRAWN & RED PEPPER CANNELLONI

SERVES 4

I find it easier to roll up sheets of lasagne, than trying to stuff cannelloni tubes.

250 g (8 oz) can red peppers, drained and finely
    chopped
125 g (4 oz) peeled prawns, chopped
125 g (4 oz) ricotta cheese
2 tablespoons fromage frais
2 teaspoons paprika
1/4 teaspoon chilli powder
salt and pepper to taste
175 g (6 oz) fresh lasagne
450 ml (3/4 pint) milk
25 g (1 oz) butter
25 g (1 oz) plain flour
50 g (2 oz) grated gruyère cheese
1 tablespoon dried wholemeal breadcrumbs
parsley sprigs to garnish

1. Preheat oven to 180°C (350°F/Gas 4). In a bowl, mix together the chopped peppers, prawns, ricotta, fromage frais, paprika, chilli and salt. Lay the lasagne sheets on a work surface. Spread a little filling along one long side of each sheet and roll up loosely, enclosing the filling. Place close together in a shallow ovenproof dish.

2. Warm the milk. Melt the butter in a small pan, stir in the flour and cook for 1 minute. Whisk in the milk, then cook, stirring, until thickened and smooth. Season.

3. Pour the sauce over the pasta and sprinkle with gruyère and breadcrumbs. Bake for 25 minutes, or until the pasta is cooked and the topping is golden brown. Garnish with parsley to serve.

BAKED HADDOCK PASTA

SERVES 4

Make this complete meal for all the family – the children will love it!

250 g (8 oz) pasta knots or twists
600 ml (1 pint) milk
40 g (1½ oz) butter
40 g (1½ oz) plain flour
freshly grated nutmeg to taste
salt and pepper to taste
500 g (1 lb) skinned smoked haddock, cubed
3 tomatoes, skinned and quartered
4 spring onions, chopped
1 tablespoon dried white breadcrumbs
50 g (2 oz) double Gloucester cheese, grated

1. Preheat oven to 180°C (350°F/Gas 4). Bring a large pan of salted water to the boil. Add the pasta, stir once and boil for 10-12 minutes until tender.

2. Meanwhile make the sauce. Warm the milk. Melt the butter in a small saucepan, stir in the flour and cook for 1 minute. Whisk in the milk and cook, stirring, until the sauce is thickened and smooth. Season with nutmeg, salt and pepper.

3. Drain the pasta and toss in a little oil to prevent sticking. Lightly mix with the haddock, tomatoes, spring onions and sauce.

4. Turn into a buttered ovenproof dish and sprinkle with the breadcrumbs and cheese. Bake for 30 minutes, until the topping is golden brown.

LEMON SOLE & LETTUCE

SERVES 4-6

Stir fried strips of sole fillet in a light lemon sauce
are served on a bed of cucumber and lettuce.
Accompany this tasty dish with rice or noodles.

1 egg white
1 tablespoon cornflour
1 tablespoon light soy sauce
1/2 teaspoon Chinese five-spice powder
salt and pepper to taste
500 g (1 lb) sole fillets, skinned
4 tablespoons groundnut oil
1 clove garlic, crushed
2.5 cm (1 inch) piece fresh root ginger, thinly
    sliced
4 spring onions, cut into 5 cm (2 inch) lengths
1/2 cucumber, halved lengthways, seeded and
    sliced
1/2 cos lettuce, shredded

SAUCE
juice of 2 lemons
1/2 teaspoon finely grated lemon rind
6 tablespoons water
2 tablespoons sherry
2 tablespoons soy sauce
1 tablespoon wine vinegar
2 tablespoons sugar
1 tablespoon cornflour

TO GARNISH
lemon slices and chives

1 Mix together all the ingredients for the sauce in
a bowl and set aside.

2 In another bowl, whisk the egg white until
frothy, then stir in the cornflour, soy sauce, five-
spice powder and seasoning.

3 Cut the sole fillets into wide strips, add to the
egg mixture and toss to coat.

4 Heat the oil in a wok. Fry fish in batches for 1
minute only on each side. Drain on kitchen
paper, transfer to a warmed serving plate and
keep warm.

5 Pour off all but 2 tablespoons oil from the wok.
Add the garlic, ginger and spring onions and stir
fry for 1 minute. Pour in the sauce mixture and stir
until thickened.

6 Stir in the cucumber and lettuce and cook for
1-2 minutes. Adjust the seasoning.

7 Spoon the vegetables and lemon sauce over the
fish and serve at once, garnished with lemon
slices and chives.

FISH WITH LEEKS & RED PEPPER

SERVES 4

If you cannot get fresh small venus clams, use a jar of clams instead. Serve this tasty dish with plenty of crusty bread for mopping up the juices.

3 tablespoons olive oil
1 clove garlic, crushed
1 celery stick, chopped
2 leeks, sliced
1 red pepper, cored, seeded and sliced
400 g (14 oz) can chopped tomatoes
150 ml (¼ pint) white wine
1 tablespoon chopped parsley
500 g (1 lb) cod or haddock fillet, skinned and diced
250 g (8 oz) mackerel fillet, diced
350 g (12 oz) clams, scrubbed
salt and pepper to taste

1 Heat the oil in a large shallow pan or wok. Add the garlic, celery, leeks and red pepper and stir fry for 3 minutes.

2 Stir in the tomatoes, white wine and 150 ml (¼ pint) water. Bring to the boil, then lower the heat and simmer for 3 minutes. Stir in the parsley, fish and clams and cook gently for about 5 minutes until the clams are open and the fish is opaque and cooked through. Season and serve immediately.

SEAFOOD WITH FENNEL & TOMATOES

SERVES 4

A delicious combination of stir fried fennel, onion and garlic with a medley of seafood.

6 tablespoons virgin olive oil
2 onions, chopped
1 small fennel bulb, sliced
2 cloves garlic, crushed
4 large tomatoes, peeled and chopped
bouquet garni
1 bay leaf
large strip of lemon peel
large pinch of powdered saffron
500 g (1 lb) mixed fish fillet, skinned and cut into bite-size pieces, e.g. monkfish, conger eel, red mullet, snapper
250 g (8 oz) raw King prawns, peeled and deveined
salt and pepper to taste

TO GARNISH
snipped chives

1 Heat 3 tablespoons of the oil in a wok or sauté pan. Add the onions, fennel and garlic and stir fry over a gentle heat, for 8 minutes.

2 Add the tomatoes, bouquet garni, bay leaf, lemon peel and saffron, with the remaining oil and 150 ml (¼ pint) boiling water. Bring to a rapid boil, then lower the heat.

3 Add the fish in stages; firmer fish such as monkfish and conger eel first, followed by the more flaky varieties such as mullet and snapper; finally add the prawns. Simmer for 5 minutes, until just cooked.

4 Season to taste and garnish with snipped chives.

ABOVE: SEAFOOD WITH FENNEL & TOMATOES *BELOW*: FISH WITH LEEKS & RED PEPPER

PENNE WITH CHORIZO & CORN

SERVES 4

I used hot chorizo sausage for this sauce; it gives a deliciously fiery taste. If you prefer a milder flavour, use sweet chorizo which is lightly spiced with paprika.

250 g (8 oz) penne
1 tablespoon olive oil
1 small onion, thinly sliced
350 g (12 oz) chorizo sausage, sliced
125 g (4 oz) baby corn
salt to taste
1 tablespoon chopped parsley

1 Bring a large saucepan of salted water to the boil. Add the penne, stir once and boil for 10-12 minutes until tender. Drain well.

2 Meanwhile make the sauce. Heat the oil in a frying pan, add the onion and fry for about 5 minutes, until lightly browned. Add the sausage and fry, stirring, for 5 minutes until turning crisp. Add the baby corn and cook for 2 minutes. Taste and add salt if necessary.

3 Mix the penne and sauce. Serve immediately, sprinkled with parsley.

TORTELLONI WITH SALAMI & SUN-DRIED TOMATOES

SERVES 4

Served with this flavoursome sauce, spinach and ricotta tortelloni provides a substantial meal. For a lighter meal or a tasty starter, serve the sauce with fine tagliatelle instead.

50 g (2 oz) sun-dried tomatoes in oil
1 tablespoon oil (from tomato jar)
2 tablespoons olive oil
2 cloves garlic, finely chopped
50 g (2 oz) Italian salami, chopped
1 teaspoon Dijon mustard
2 tablespoons chopped parsley
1 tablespoon lemon juice
350 g (12 oz) spinach & ricotta tortelloni
parsley sprigs to garnish

1 Chop the sun-dried tomatoes into small pieces, then place in a saucepan with the oils, garlic, salami, mustard, parsley and lemon juice. Mix well and leave to marinade for a few minutes.

2 Bring a large saucepan of salted water to the boil. Add the tortelloni, stir once and boil for 12-15 minutes until tender. Halfway through the cooking time, warm the sauce through gently.

3 Drain the pasta and return it to the pan. Add the sauce, toss well and serve immediately, garnished with parsley.

CHICKEN RISOTTO

SERVES 4

This Venetian risotto should have a creamy consistency. I sometimes make it with leftover chicken, in which case I mix the chicken into the rice with the olives.

3 tablespoons olive oil
350 g (12 oz) boneless chicken breast, skinned
    and cut into 2.5 cm (1 inch) cubes
1 onion, chopped
2 cloves garlic, chopped
300 g (10 oz) Italian risotto rice
600 ml (1 pint) chicken stock
150 ml (¼ pint) white wine
225 ml (8 fl oz) passata
2 teaspoons chopped oregano or ½ teaspoon
    dried
salt and pepper to taste
50 g (2 oz) black olives, halved and stoned
2 sun dried tomatoes, sliced
50 g (2 oz) Parmesan cheese, shredded

TO GARNISH
oregano sprigs

1 Heat the oil in a heavy based pan, add the chicken, onion and garlic and fry, stirring, for 5 minutes.

2 Add the rice, stock, wine, passata, oregano and seasoning, and bring to the boil.

3 Cover and cook gently for 25 minutes until the liquid is absorbed and the rice is just tender.

4 Remove from the heat and fork in the olives and sun dried tomatoes. Turn into a heated serving dish and sprinkle with the Parmesan. Garnish with oregano to serve.

SPAGHETTI WITH DOLCELATTE & CHICKEN

SERVES 4

350 g (12 oz) spaghetti
150 ml (¼ pint) soured cream
125 g (4 oz) dolcelatte, chopped
3 tablespoons chopped chives
125 g (4 oz) cooked chicken, chopped
salt and pepper to taste

TO GARNISH
chives

1 Bring a large pan of salted water to the boil. Add the spaghetti, stir once and boil for 10-12 minutes until tender.

2 Drain the spaghetti thoroughly, then return to the pan. Add the soured cream, dolcelatte, chives, chicken and seasoning. Heat through very gently, stirring constantly.

3 Serve immediately, garnished with chives and accompanied by a green salad.

BEEF WITH MINT & CASHEWS

SERVES 4

The coolness of the mint counteracts the fire of the chilli in this stir fry of rump steak and cashew nuts.

2 tablespoons groundnut oil
1 clove garlic, crushed
500 g (1 lb) rump steak, cut into thin strips
1-2 red chillis, seeded and sliced
4 spring onions, sliced
2.5 cm (1 inch) piece fresh root ginger, grated
3 tablespoons dark soy sauce
2 tablespoons sherry
2 tablespoons chopped mint
50 g (2 oz) salted cashew nuts
pepper to taste

TO GARNISH
mint sprigs

1 Heat the oil in a wok. Add the garlic and steak strips and stir fry over a high heat for 1-2 minutes to seal.

2 Add the chillis, spring onions and ginger and stir fry for 1 minute.

3 Add the remaining ingredients and continue stir frying for 1 minute. Season with pepper and serve at once, garnished with mint.

BEEF WITH PEPPERS & NOODLES

SERVES 4

A delicious dish with a Thai influence. If time, pop the beef in the freezer for 30 minutes before cutting; you will find it easier to slice into wafer-thin strips.

250 g (8 oz) egg noodles
2 tablespoons groundnut oil
350 g (12 oz) fillet steak, cut into thin strips
1 small red pepper, cored, seeded and cut into
    julienne strips
1 small yellow pepper, cored, seeded and cut into
    julienne strips
salt and pepper to taste

HOT PASTE
2 garlic cloves, chopped
5 cm (2 inch) piece fresh root ginger, chopped
3 stalks lemon grass, bulb end only, chopped
    (optional)
2 tablespoons groundnut oil
1 teaspoon sesame oil
2 tablespoons soy sauce
3 tablespoons sweet chilli sauce

1 Put all the ingredients for the hot paste in a blender or food processor and process until fairly smooth; or use a pestle and mortar. Set aside.

2 Cook the noodles in boiling water according to packet instructions and drain well.

3 Meanwhile heat the oil in a wok. Add the beef and peppers and stir fry for 3 minutes. Remove from the wok and set aside.

4 Add the hot paste to the wok and cook for 1-2 minutes. Add the noodles, with the beef and pepper mixture, and seasoning. Toss well and heat through. Serve at once.

ABOVE: BEEF WITH PEPPERS & NOODLES *BELOW*: BEEF WITH MINT & CASHEWS

PORK FILLET WITH BABY CORN

SERVES 4

Tenderloin of pork is superb for stir fry recipes. It is easily sliced into thin, even pieces and is so tender it needs only the shortest cooking time. Serve this dish with rice, noodles or new potatoes, and a green vegetable or leafy salad.

500 g (1 lb) pork fillet (tenderloin)
1½ tablespoons green peppercorns in brine, drained
3 tablespoons groundnut oil
1 shallot, finely chopped
1 clove garlic, crushed
175 g (6 oz) baby corn cobs, halved lengthwise
2 tablespoons brandy or dry vermouth
4 tablespoons double cream
salt to taste

TO GARNISH
mint sprigs

1 Cut the pork into thin slices. Lightly crush the green peppercorns using a pestle and mortar or rolling pin. Set aside.

2 Heat the oil in a wok or large frying pan. Add the pork and stir fry over a high heat for 1 minute. Add the shallot and garlic and continue stir frying for 2 minutes.

3 Add the corn cobs to the wok and stir fry for 1-2 minutes until they are almost tender. Stir in the crushed peppercorns, brandy or vermouth. Cook over a high heat until the juices are reduced to about 1 tablespoon. Lower the heat and stir in the cream. Season with salt and serve immediately, garnished with mint sprigs.

PORK WITH WATER CHESTNUTS

SERVES 4

If you have time, do allow the pork and water chestnuts to mingle with the flavours of the ginger, garlic and soy before cooking. Water chestnuts have a wonderful crunchy texture and although they have little taste of their own they readily absorb the flavours of the marinade.

350 g (12 oz) pork tenderloin
170 g (6 oz) can water chestnuts, drained and sliced
1 clove garlic, crushed
2.5 cm (1 inch) piece fresh root ginger, grated
2 tablespoons Worcestershire sauce
2 tablespoons soy sauce
½ head Chinese leaf, shredded
1 tablespoon chopped coriander leaves
2 teaspoons snipped chives
5 tablespoons light olive oil
1 red pepper, cored, seeded and cut into strips
2 tablespoons sherry or wine vinegar
½ teaspoon dark soft brown sugar
salt and pepper to taste

1 Slice the pork thinly and place in a bowl with the water chestnuts. Add the garlic, ginger, Worcestershire and soy sauces and stir well to coat. Leave to marinate for 20 minutes, or longer.

2 In another bowl toss the Chinese leaf with the chopped coriander leaves and the chives. Arrange on individual plates.

3 Heat 3 tablespoons oil in a wok. Add the pork mixture and stir fry over a high heat to seal. Add the red pepper and continue cooking for a further 2 minutes, until the pork is cooked through. Stir in the remaining oil, vinegar, sugar and seasoning. Spoon over the Chinese leaf and serve.

ABOVE: PORK WITH WATER CHESTNUTS *BELOW*: PORK FILLET WITH BABY CORN

CHICKEN FRICASSÉE

SERVES 4

A very useful recipe for using up leftover chicken or turkey. You can also add sliced green or red peppers, peas or sweetcorn, for a change.

40 g (1½ oz) butter
1 onion, chopped
175 g (6 oz) mushrooms, sliced
½ teaspoon paprika
25 g (1 oz) flour
300 ml (½ pint) chicken stock
350 g (12 oz) cooked chicken, cut into chunks
120 ml (4 fl oz) single cream
salt and pepper to taste
1 tablespoon chopped chervil or parsley
chervil or parsley sprigs to garnish

1 Heat the butter in a pan and fry the onion until softened. Add the mushrooms and cook for a further 2 minutes.

2 Stir in the paprika and flour and cook for 30 seconds, then gradually stir in the stock. Bring to the boil and cook, stirring, for 2 minutes, until thickened.

3 Add the chicken, cream and seasoning, and heat gently for a few minutes.

4 Turn into a serving dish and sprinkle with chopped chervil or parsley. Garnish with sprigs of chervil or parsley and serve with boiled rice.

MEDITERRANEAN CHICKEN

SERVES 4

A rich sauce of peppers, tomatoes and olives cooked with goujons of chicken. Sun dried tomatoes enhance the Mediterranean flavour.

3 tablespoons olive oil
1 small onion, thinly sliced
350 g (12 oz) chicken goujons
2 cloves garlic, chopped
1 small red pepper, cored, seeded and thinly sliced
1 small green pepper, cored, seeded and thinly sliced
400 g (14 oz) can chopped tomatoes
4 sun dried tomatoes in oil, drained and thinly sliced
50 g (2 oz) black olives, halved and stoned
salt and pepper to taste
2 tablespoons chopped basil
basil sprigs to garnish

1 Heat the oil in a heavy based pan and fry the onion and chicken together, stirring occasionally, until the chicken is sealed.

2 Add the garlic and peppers, and cook for a further 4 minutes, stirring occasionally.

3 Add the chopped tomatoes, sun dried tomatoes, olives and seasoning. Cover and cook for 5 minutes.

4 Stir in the basil. Serve garnished with sprigs of basil and accompanied by rice or crusty bread.

CHICKEN MASALA

SERVES 4

A delicious, mild curry – best served with plain boiled basmati rice and mango chutney. I often make it with leftover cooked chicken – simply cut into chunks and add to the coconut sauce, reducing the cooking time to 5 minutes.

2 tablespoons sunflower oil
500 g (1 lb) boneless chicken breast, skinned and
    cut into cubes
1 onion, chopped
2 cloves garlic, crushed
½ teaspoon ground cumin
1 teaspoon ground coriander
1 teaspoon turmeric
seeds from 4 cardamom pods
2 teaspoons finely chopped fresh root ginger
25 g (1 oz) creamed coconut, blended with
    185 ml (6 fl oz) boiling water
salt to taste
150 ml (¼ pint) double cream
1 tablespoon chopped coriander leaves

TO GARNISH
coriander sprigs

1 Heat the oil in a heavy based pan, add the chicken and fry, stirring, until sealed all over. Remove from the pan.

2 Add the onion to the pan and fry until softened, then add the garlic, spices and ginger; fry for 1 minute, stirring constantly.

3 Return the chicken to the pan. Add the coconut liquid with salt. Cover and simmer for 15 minutes.

4 Stir in the cream and chopped coriander and cook for 3 minutes. Serve with rice, garnished with coriander sprigs.

TURKEY CHILLI

SERVES 4

Turkey mince is quick to cook and available from most supermarkets. Add more chilli powder if you like a really hot chilli.

2 tablespoons olive oil
1 onion, chopped
500 g (1 lb) minced turkey
2 cloves garlic, chopped
¼ teaspoon chilli powder
1 teaspoon ground cumin
1 tablespoon flour
120 ml (4 fl oz) chicken stock
175 g (6 oz) can red peppers, drained and sliced
400 g (14 oz) can chopped tomatoes
1 tablespoon tomato purée
salt and pepper to taste
2 x 400 g (14 oz) cans red kidney beans, drained
1 tablespoon chopped parsley

1 Heat the oil in a pan, add the onion and fry until softened. Add the turkey and garlic and fry briskly, stirring, until sealed all over.

2 Add the spices and flour and cook, stirring, for 1 minute. Stir in the stock, red peppers, tomatoes, tomato purée and seasoning, and bring to the boil.

3 Cover and cook for 20 minutes, then stir in the beans and parsley and heat through.

BAKED MACARONI WITH MEAT SAUCE

SERVES 4

This dish can be completely assembled several hours before you wish to serve it, in which case the baking time must be increased to 25 minutes.

---

1 tablespoon olive oil
1 clove garlic, crushed
4 rashers smoked streaky bacon, derinded and
    chopped
1 small onion, chopped
250 g (8 oz) lean minced lamb
salt and pepper to taste
½ teaspoon dried marjoram
2 tablespoons chopped parsley
125 ml (4 fl oz) dry white wine
250 g (8 oz) passata
250 g (8 oz) macaroni

SAUCE
300 ml (½ pint) milk
25 g (1 oz) butter
25 g (1 oz) plain flour
freshly grated nutmeg to taste

TO FINISH
125 g (4 oz) gruyère cheese, grated
thyme sprigs to garnish

1 Preheat oven to 200°C (400°F/Gas 6). Heat the oil in a saucepan. Add the garlic, bacon and onion and fry for about 5 minutes, until the onion is lightly browned. Add the lamb and fry, stirring, until evenly coloured. Add the salt, pepper, herbs, wine and passata and bring to the boil. Simmer, uncovered, for about 20 minutes, stirring occasionally.

2 Meanwhile, bring a large saucepan of salted water to the boil. Add the macaroni, stir once and boil for 10-12 minutes until tender.

3 To make the sauce, heat the milk. Melt the butter in a small saucepan, stir in the flour and cook for 1 minute. Add the milk all at once and bring to the boil, whisking all the time, until the sauce is thickened and smooth. Season with salt, pepper and nutmeg.

4 Drain the macaroni and spread half of it in a buttered ovenproof dish. Pour over half of the meat sauce. Cover with the remaining macaroni, then the rest of the meat sauce. Top with the white sauce and sprinkle with cheese.

5 Bake in the oven for 15 minutes, until bubbling and golden brown. If the top is not sufficiently browned, place under a preheated hot grill for 2-3minutes. Garnish with thyme to serve.

CALVES LIVER WITH MUSTARD SEEDS & ROSEMARY

SERVES 4

A simple dish of calves liver and onion flavoured with mustard and rosemary. Take care to avoid overcooking the liver or its creamy texture will be lost – it should be just pink on the inside. Serve with new potatoes and french beans, or pasta and a crisp green salad.

500 g (1 lb) calves liver, thinly sliced
salt and pepper to taste
2 tablespoons olive oil
25 g (1 oz) butter
1 shallot, chopped
1 small onion, sliced
4-5 teaspoons mustard seeds
2 tablespoons finely chopped rosemary

TO GARNISH
rosemary sprigs

1 Season the liver with salt and pepper. Heat the oil and half of the butter in a large frying pan. Add the liver slices and cook for 2-3 minutes each side. Transfer to a serving dish using a slotted spoon and keep warm.

2 Add the shallot and onion to the pan juices and cook for 3 minutes to soften. Add the remaining butter, mustard seeds and chopped rosemary and heat until sizzling. Spoon over the liver and serve at once, garnished with rosemary sprigs.

MEATBALLS IN CREAM & HERB SAUCE

SERVES 4

MEATBALLS
350 g (12 oz) lean minced beef, or veal
125 g (4 oz) back bacon, derinded and chopped
1 small onion, very finely chopped
2 cloves garlic, crushed
125 g (4 oz) pitted black olives
1 tablespoon chopped parsley
1 tablespoon Worcestershire sauce
1 egg yolk
salt and pepper to taste

TO FINISH
1½ tablespoons olive oil
25 g (1 oz) butter
5 tablespoons light stock
3 tablespoons chopped mixed herbs, e.g. parsley and fennel
5 tablespoons double cream

TO GARNISH
fennel or parsley sprigs

1 In a large bowl, mix together all the ingredients for the meatballs. Shape into small balls.

2 Heat the oil and butter in a large frying pan and fry the meatballs, turning constantly, for about 5 minutes until evenly browned. Remove from pan.

3 Add the stock and herbs to the pan, stirring to scrape up any sediment. Cook over a high heat until reduced to about 3 tablespoons. Stir in the cream and seasoning.

4 Return the meatballs to the pan and cook gently for 3-5 minutes. Serve garnished with fennel and accompanied by noodles.

LAMB WITH CORIANDER & LIME

SERVES 4

You can make this very simple stir fry either with loin or neck lamb fillet. Neck fillet is less expensive and readily available, but not as lean and tender as loin. Serve with rice.

3 tablespoons virgin olive oil
350 g (12 oz) fillet of lamb, sliced
1-2 cloves garlic, crushed
¼ teaspoon ground cumin
1 onion, cut into wedges
juice of 2 limes
150 g (5 oz) natural yogurt
3 tablespoons chopped coriander leaves
½ teaspoon sugar
salt and pepper to taste

TO GARNISH
lime slices and coriander leaves

1. Heat the oil in a wok or large frying pan. Add the lamb and garlic and stir fry for 1 minute to seal. Add the cumin and onion and stir fry for 2 minutes.

2. Add the remaining ingredients to the pan. Cook, stirring, for 2-3 minutes until the lamb is tender.

3. Season and serve at once, garnished with lime slices and coriander.

LAMB WITH CHICK PEAS & MINT

SERVES 4

To ensure that this dish is richly flavoured and not too liquid, reduce the sauce right down. Serve with rice or naan bread, or both.

3 tablespoons olive oil
500 g (1 lb) lean leg of lamb, diced
2 onions, chopped
2 cloves garlic, crushed
1 green chilli, seeded and chopped
2 teaspoons coriander seeds, lightly crushed
1 teaspoon cumin seeds, lightly crushed
¼ teaspoon ground allspice
½ teaspoon turmeric
300 ml (½ pint) hot lamb stock
400 g (14 oz) can chick peas, drained
2 tomatoes, skinned and quartered
2 tablespoons chopped mint
salt and pepper to taste

TO SERVE
mint sprigs to garnish
thick natural yogurt

1. Heat the oil in a wok or large sauté pan. Add the lamb and stir fry for about 4 minutes until sealed and browned. Add the onions, garlic, chilli and spices and cook, stirring, for 3 minutes.

2. Add the stock and chick peas to the pan and bring to the boil. Lower the heat, cover and simmer for about 20 minutes until the lamb is tender.

3. Remove the lid and continue cooking until most of the liquid is evaporated. Stir in the tomatoes, mint and seasoning. Cook for a further 2 minutes. Serve garnished with mint and accompanied by rice and thick yogurt.

SPICED RICE WITH OKRA & CHICKEN

SERVES 4

When buying okra choose small bright green pods, about 7.5-10 cm (3-4 inches) long. Salting and draining removes their sticky gum.

175 g (6 oz) okra
2 teaspoons salt
1 boneless chicken breast, skinned and diced
1 tablespoon Worcestershire sauce
few drops of Tabasco sauce
1 clove garlic, crushed
¼ teaspoon celery seed
4 tablespoons olive oil
75 g (3 oz) frozen sweetcorn kernels, thawed
250 g (8 oz) white rice, cooked
salt and pepper to taste

1 Top and tail the okra, slice into rings and place in a colander or sieve. Rinse well and sprinkle with the salt. Leave to drain for 15 minutes, then rinse thoroughly to remove the salt. Dry on kitchen paper.

2 Meanwhile, mix together the chicken, Worcestershire sauce, Tabasco, garlic and celery seed.

3 Heat the oil in a wok. Add the chicken mixture and stir fry for 1 minute. Add the okra and continue stir frying for 1 minute, then add the sweetcorn and cook for a further 1 minute.

4 Fold in the rice and heat through, stirring to prevent sticking. Season and serve immediately.

SWEET & SOUR NOODLES

SERVES 4

250 g (8 oz) thread egg noodles
3 tablespoons groundnut oil
1 clove garlic, crushed
2.5 cm (1 inch) piece fresh root ginger, grated
1 small leek, sliced
1 carrot, cut into strips
125 g (4 oz) baby corn cobs, halved
½ red pepper, cut into diamonds
2 tomatoes, cut into wedges
1 tablespoon chopped coriander leaves
salt and pepper to taste

SAUCE
3 tablespoons soy sauce
3 tablespoons wine vinegar
3 tablespoons sherry
3 tablespoons soft light brown sugar
6 tablespoons pineapple juice
1 teaspoon cornflour

TO GARNISH
coriander sprigs

1 Mix all the ingredients for the sauce together in a small bowl. Set aside. Cook the noodles according to packet instructions.

2 Heat the oil in a wok. Add the garlic, ginger, leek, carrot, baby corn and red pepper and stir fry over a high heat for 2 minutes.

3 Add the sauce and stir until thickened. Lower the heat and simmer for 2 minutes.

4 Drain the noodles and add to the wok with the tomato wedges and coriander. Toss gently and season. Serve immediately, garnished with coriander.

GREEK LAMB WITH ORZO

SERVES 4-5

Orzo – also called puntalette – is tiny pasta shaped like rice grains. It soaks up all the delicious cooking juices. Although the cooking time is long, it is assembled in minutes and needs little attention.

750 g (1½ lb) boneless lamb
2 onions, sliced
2 tablespoons lemon juice
salt and pepper to taste
1 tablespoon chopped oregano
1 teaspoon ground cumin
½ teaspoon ground cinnamon
1 tablespoon olive oil
2 tablespoons tomato purée
900 ml (1½ pints) boiling water
250 g (8 oz) orzo

TO SERVE
oregano leaves to garnish
freshly shredded Parmesan cheese

1 Preheat oven to 180°C (350°F/Gas 4). Cut the lamb into 4 cm (1½ inch) cubes and place in a large casserole dish. Add the onions, lemon juice, seasoning, oregano, cumin and cinnamon. Mix well, then drizzle over the oil. Bake, uncovered, for 1 hour.

2 Mix together the tomato purée and boiling water and pour over the lamb. Cover and cook in the oven for 30 minutes.

3 Add the orzo, stir well, then cover and return to the oven for 30 minutes. Serve sprinkled with oregano leaves and Parmesan.

PENNE WITH RICH SAUSAGE SAUCE

SERVES 4-6

Choose good quality Italian or Cumberland sausages for this dish.

500 g (1 lb) sausages, skins removed
2 tablespoons olive oil
1 onion, thinly sliced
150 ml (¼ pint) red wine
397 g (14 oz) can chopped tomatoes
1 tablespoon tomato purée
125 g (4 oz) mushrooms, sliced
salt and pepper to taste
250-350 g (8-12 oz) penne
25 g (1 oz) butter
2 tablespoons freshly grated Parmesan cheese
herb sprigs to garnish

1 Shape each sausage into 4-5 small balls. Heat the oil in a deep frying pan, add the meatballs and fry until evenly browned, about 5 minutes. Spoon off any excess oil, leaving a little in the pan, then add the onion and fry for 5 minutes.

2 Add the wine, tomatoes, tomato purée, mushrooms, salt and pepper. Bring to the boil, stirring gently. Lower the heat, cover and simmer for 15-20 minutes.

3 Meanwhile bring a large pan of salted water to the boil. Add the pasta, stir once and boil for 10-12 minutes until tender.

4 Drain the pasta thoroughly, then return to the pan, add the butter and Parmesan and stir over a low heat until the butter has melted. Serve piping hot, topped with the sausage sauce and herbs.

ABOVE: GREEK LAMB WITH ORZO *BELOW*: PENNE WITH RICH SAUSAGE SAUCE

PASTA WITH COURGETTES & 'BACON'

SERVES 4

A great dish if you are in a hurry, as it uses few ingredients and is cooked in minutes. Pancetta – Italian cured pork – is ideal for this. It is similar in taste to a mild cured bacon, which is a good substitute.

250 g (8 oz) ondule or pasta shells
3 tablespoons olive oil
125 g (4 oz) pancetta or mild streaky bacon, chopped
175 g (6 oz) courgettes, shredded
1-2 tablespoons lemon juice
salt and pepper to taste
good handful of basil leaves

1 Bring a large saucepan of salted water to the boil. Coil in the ondule or add the pasta shells and boil for 10-12 minutes until tender.

2 Meanwhile, heat 1 tablespoon oil in a large saucepan, add the pancetta or bacon and fry for 5 minutes, or until slightly crisp. Add the remaining oil and when hot, add the courgettes and stir well. Lower the heat, cover and cook for 2 minutes.

3 Stir in the lemon juice, pepper and half of the basil leaves, torn if large. Simmer for 2 minutes. Taste and add salt if necessary.

4 Drain the cooked pasta thoroughly and add to the sauce ingredients. Stir well and serve immediately, garnished with the remaining basil.

TAGLIATELLE WITH PROSCIUTTO & VEGETABLE RIBBONS

SERVES 4

For an economical alternative, use cooked ham instead of prosciutto.

125 g (4 oz) prosciutto
2 carrots
2-3 courgettes
250-350 g (8-12 oz) fresh or dried tagliatelle
50 g (2 oz) butter
50 g (2 oz) freshly grated Parmesan cheese
pepper to taste

1 Cut the prosciutto into thin strips. Using a potato peeler, pare the carrots and courgettes lengthwise into ribbons.

2 Bring a large saucepan of salted water to the boil. Add the pasta, stir once and boil for 4-5 minutes for fresh pasta; 8-10 minutes for dried.

3 Meanwhile make the sauce. Melt the butter in a frying pan, add the prosciutto and stir-fry for 1 minute. Add the vegetable ribbons and stir-fry for 2-3 minutes.

4 Drain the pasta and place in a large warmed dish. Add the vegetable mixture, Parmesan and plenty of pepper. Stir well, tossing all the ingredients together. Serve immediately.

PENNE WITH FONTINA & TARRAGON SAUCE

SERVES 4

Fontina cheese is used in Italy to make fonduta – the Italian version of a fondue. It melts very easily and has a creamy taste with a sharp tang. Add some lightly cooked sliced mushrooms before serving, if you like.

250-350 g (8-12 oz) penne
150 ml (¼ pint) milk
125 g (4 oz) fontina cheese, cubed
1 egg yolk
1 tablespoon tarragon leaves
salt and pepper to taste
tarragon sprigs to garnish
freshly grated Parmesan cheese to serve

1 Bring a large saucepan of salted water to the boil. Add the pasta, stir once and boil for 10-12 minutes until tender.

2 Meanwhile make the sauce. Warm the milk, then pour into a small bowl over a pan of simmering water. Add the cheese and egg yolk and cook, stirring occasionally, until the sauce is smooth. Do not overheat or the egg will curdle. Stir in the tarragon and pepper. Taste and add salt if necessary.

3 Drain the pasta and mix with the sauce. Transfer to individual bowls. Garnish with tarragon and sprinkle with Parmesan and pepper to serve.

PASTA WHEELS WITH MASCARPONE & PECAN SAUCE

SERVES 4

Mascarpone is a fresh Italian cream cheese sold in tubs. Substitute cream cheese or curd cheese if you can't find it.

250-350 g (8-12 oz) pasta wheels
125 g (4 oz) mascarpone cheese
150 ml (¼ pint) single cream
1 tablespoon freshly grated Parmesan cheese
salt and pepper to taste
1 teaspoon chopped marjoram
a little milk (optional)
1 tablespoon olive oil
1 tablespoon lemon juice
25 g (1 oz) shelled pecan nuts, chopped
marjoram sprigs to garnish

1 Bring a large saucepan of salted water to the boil. Add the pasta, stir once and boil for 10-12 minutes until tender.

2 Meanwhile make the sauce. Heat the mascarpone gently in a small saucepan until melted. Add the cream, Parmesan, salt, pepper and marjoram and heat through gently. Add a little milk if the sauce seems too thick.

3 Drain the pasta and toss in the oil and lemon juice. Divide the pasta between warmed plates and pour over the sauce. Sprinkle with nuts and marjoram. Serve immediately.

ABOVE: PENNE WITH FONTINA & TARRAGON SAUCE BELOW: PASTA WITH MASCARPONE & PECAN SAUCE

RIGATONI WITH TOMATO & EGG SAUCE

SERVES 4

Including eggs in this tomato sauce gives a rich, creamy texture and taste. A great spur of the moment meal, as you are likely to have the ingredients at home.

2 tablespoons olive oil
25 g (1 oz) butter
1 onion, chopped
397 g (14 oz) carton passata
salt and pepper to taste
350 g (12 oz) rigatoni
2 eggs, beaten
2 tablespoons freshly grated Parmesan cheese
10-12 basil leaves, torn if large

1 Heat the oil and butter in a pan, add the onion and fry gently for 5 minutes, until softened. Add the passata and seasoning. Bring to the boil and simmer, uncovered, for 12-15 minutes until thickened.

2 Meanwhile bring a large pan of salted water to the boil. Add the pasta, stir once and boil for 10-12 minutes until tender. Drain and return to the pan. Keep warm.

3 To finish the sauce, lower the heat to a gentle simmer, then slowly pour in the eggs, stirring all the time, until the sauce is thickened and creamy; do not allow to boil. Stir in half of the Parmesan and basil. Check seasoning.

4 Pour the sauce over the pasta. Sprinkle with the remaining Parmesan and basil to serve.

SHELLS WITH RICOTTA & TOMATO SAUCE

SERVES 4

These giant shells look most interesting nestling in their sauce. If time is really short, use one of the ready-made tomato sauces now available instead of making your own.

250 g (8 oz) large pasta shells
350 g (12 oz) ricotta cheese
1 egg, beaten
2 tablespoons chopped basil
3 tablespoons freshly grated Parmesan cheese
salt and pepper to taste
1 quantity fresh tomato sauce
basil sprigs to garnish

1 Preheat oven to 180°C (350°F/Gas 4). Bring a large saucepan of salted water to the boil. Add the pasta, stir once and boil for 8 minutes; drain well.

2 Meanwhile, in a bowl mix together the ricotta, egg, basil, half of the Parmesan, salt and pepper.

3 Spoon the stuffing into the shells and arrange in a buttered shallow ovenproof dish. Pour the sauce over the shells and sprinkle with the remaining Parmesan. Bake for 25 minutes, until the topping is golden brown.

4 Serve immediately, garnished with basil.

ORECCHIETTE WITH SMOKED TROUT

SERVES 4

For this recipe buy pieces of smoked trout fillet from the chilled counter, not the smoked trout which is prepared and packed like smoked salmon.

250 g (8 oz) orecchiette
½ bunch watercress
125 g (4 oz) smoked trout fillet
125 g (4 oz) curd cheese
2 teaspoons coarse-grain mustard
2 tablespoons dry white wine
150 ml (¼ pint) single cream
salt and pepper to taste
freshly shredded Parmesan cheese to serve

1 Bring a large pan of salted water to the boil. Add the pasta, stir once and boil for 10-12 minutes until tender.

2 Meanwhile make the sauce. Chop the watercress roughly. Cut the trout into small strips. Place the curd cheese, mustard, wine and cream in a small saucepan and heat gently, stirring, until thickened and smooth. Add the watercress, trout, salt and pepper; heat through gently for 2-3 minutes.

3 Drain the pasta and mix with the sauce, tossing thoroughly. Serve sprinkled with shreds of Parmesan cheese.

RIGATONI WITH BROCCOLI & ANCHOVIES

SERVES 4

I have based this recipe on one from Sicily, where broccoli and anchovy are a popular combination.

250-350 g (8-12 oz) rigatoni
4 tablespoons olive oil
2 cloves garlic, chopped
25 g (1 oz) pine nuts
50 g (1¾ oz) can anchovies
350 g (12 oz) broccoli, cut into small florets
¼ teaspoon chilli powder

1 Bring a large pan of salted water to the boil. Add the pasta, stir once and boil for 10-12 minutes until tender. Drain well.

2 Meanwhile, make the sauce. Heat the oil in a frying pan, add the garlic and pine nuts and fry for a few minutes, until the nuts are lightly browned. Chop the anchovies and add to the pan, together with their oil. Heat gently, mashing the anchovies into the oil until they start to dissolve.

3 Add the broccoli and stir well. Cover and cook gently for 5 minutes, until just tender. Add the chilli powder, taste and add salt if necessary.

4 Mix the sauce with the drained pasta and serve.

FETTUCINE WITH SUMMER VEGETABLES

SERVES 4

Use the first tender summer vegetables to make this delicate pasta dish.

25 g (1 oz) butter
1 tablespoon sunflower oil
1 clove garlic, chopped
175 g (6 oz) courgettes, cut into sticks
125 g (4 oz) thin asparagus, in pieces
125 g (4 oz) baby carrots
175 g (6 oz) tomatoes, skinned, seeded and
  quartered
125 ml (4 fl oz) dry white wine
1 tablespoon lemon juice
salt and pepper to taste
250-350 g (8-12 oz) fettucine
125 g (4 oz) mangetout or sugar snap peas
3 tablespoons double cream
freshly grated Parmesan cheese to serve

1 Heat the butter and oil in a saucepan, add the garlic and fry briefly. Add the courgettes, asparagus, carrots and tomatoes and cook for 5 minutes, stirring occasionally. Add the wine, lemon juice and seasoning. Bring to the boil, cover and cook gently for 10 minutes.

2 Meanwhile, bring a large saucepan of salted water to the boil. Add the fettucine, stir once and boil for 8 minutes. Add the mangetout and cook for 1 minute. Stir in the cream and warm through.

3 Drain the pasta, toss with the sauce and serve with grated Parmesan.

LASAGNE PARCELS WITH SPRING VEGETABLES

SERVES 4

500 g (1 lb) spinach
1 courgette, grated
1 carrot, grated
125 g (4 oz) ricotta or curd cheese
125 g (4 oz) mascarpone or cream cheese
4 tablespoons freshly grated Parmesan cheese
1 egg, beaten
salt and pepper to taste
freshly grated nutmeg to taste
250 g (8 oz) fresh lasagne
150 ml (¼ pint) single cream
150 ml (¼ pint) milk
25 g (1 oz) butter
parsley sprigs and lemon slices to garnish

1 Preheat the oven to 180°C (350°F/Gas 4). Place the spinach in a saucepan with just the water clinging to the leaves after washing and cook, covered for 5 minutes, until tender. Drain well and chop finely.

2 In a bowl, mix together the spinach, courgette, carrot, ricotta, mascarpone, 2 tablespoons Parmesan, the egg, seasoning and nutmeg.

3 Spread a little filling over each sheet of lasagne, then tuck in the ends and roll up like a parcel. Place in a single layer in a buttered shallow ovenproof dish.

4 Heat together the cream and milk and pour evenly over the lasagne. Dot with butter and sprinkle with the remaining Parmesan. Bake, uncovered, for 30 minutes, until golden brown. Garnish with parsley and lemon slices. Serve with a salad.

SPAGHETTI WITH
WALNUT & PARSLEY SAUCE

SERVES 4

This is an English version of pesto, using easily available ingredients. Wholemeal spaghetti is very good with this sauce.

25 g (1 oz) shelled walnuts
1 clove garlic, crushed
15 g (½ oz) parsley
3 tablespoons freshly grated Parmesan cheese
150 ml (¼ pint) extra virgin olive oil
salt and pepper to taste
250-350 g (8-12 oz) spaghetti
parsley sprigs to garnish

1 Place the walnuts, garlic and parsley in a blender or clean coffee grinder and chop finely. Add the Parmesan and mix well. Gradually add the oil until well blended. Taste and season with salt and pepper.

2 Bring a large saucepan of salted water to the boil. Add the spaghetti, stir once and boil for 10-12 minutes until tender. Drain and return to the pan. And the sauce and warm through, stirring well. Serve immediately, garnished with parsley.

TRENETTE WITH
FRENCH BEANS & PESTO

SERVES 4

You need to use fresh pesto for this recipe; see page 10 for a quick version. If trenette is not available use tagliatelle instead.

250 g (8 oz) French beans, cut into short lengths
salt and pepper to taste
250-350 g (8-12 oz) fresh trenette
4 tablespoons pesto
2 tablespoons olive oil
freshly shredded Parmesan to serve
basil leaves to garnish

1 Cook the French beans in a large saucepan containing plenty of boiling salted water for 10 minutes. Add the pasta, return to the boil and cook for 2-3 minutes until the pasta is tender.

2 Meanwhile warm the pesto with the oil in a small saucepan. Drain the pasta, adding 3-4 tablespoons of the cooking liquid to the pesto.

3 Toss the pasta with the pesto and serve sprinkled with Parmesan and freshly ground pepper. Garnish with basil leaves.

CHICKEN & VEGETABLE CANNELLONI

SERVES 4

Fresh lasagne is quick-cooking and easy to use. Here it encloses a light fresh-tasting chicken filling. A great supper dish, perfect served with a simple crisp salad.

350 g (12 oz) boneless chicken breasts
2 carrots, finely chopped
2 sticks celery, finely chopped
2 shallots, finely chopped
bouquet garni
150 ml (¼ pint) vegetable stock
150 ml (¼ pint) white wine
salt and pepper to taste
125 g (4 oz) curd cheese
2 teaspoons chopped marjoram
1 tablespoon lemon juice
300 g (10 oz) fresh lasagne
300 ml (½ pint) milk (approximately)
25 g (1 oz) butter
25 g (1 oz) plain flour
2 tablespoons freshly grated Parmesan cheese

1. Preheat oven to 190°C (375°F/Gas 5). Cut the chicken into 2.5 cm (1 inch) chunks and place in a saucepan with the carrots, celery, shallots and bouquet garni. Add the stock, wine, salt and pepper. Bring to the boil, cover and simmer for 15 minutes, or until the chicken is tender.

2. Strain the chicken and vegetables, reserving the stock. Discard the bouquet garni.

3. Place the chicken and vegetables in a food processor with 2 tablespoons of the stock. Process until the chicken is finely chopped, then add the curd cheese, marjoram and lemon juice. Process for a few seconds until evenly mixed. Taste and adjust seasoning if necessary.

4. Cut each sheet of lasagne in half, spread with a little of the chicken filling and roll up.

5. Make the stock up to 450 ml (¾ pint) with milk and heat gently. Melt the butter in a saucepan, add the flour and cook for 1 minute. Add the warmed liquid and bring to the boil, whisking all the time, until the sauce is thickened and smooth. Season with salt and pepper.

6. Spread a thin layer of sauce over the base of a buttered shallow oblong ovenproof dish. Arrange the pasta rolls on top, a little apart, then pour over the remaining sauce. Sprinkle with Parmesan and bake in the oven for 25-30 minutes until golden brown. Serve with a salad.

BOWS WITH GORGONZOLA & PISTACHIO SAUCE

SERVES 4

This interesting combination of warm flavours makes a great starter on a cold day and it is certainly one of my favourites.

250-350 g (8-12 oz) pasta bows
50 g (2 oz) unsalted butter
125 g (4 oz) gorgonzola cheese, cubed
150 ml (¼ pint) single cream
1 tablespoon brandy
25 g (1 oz) shelled pistachio nuts, chopped
salt and pepper to taste

1 Bring a large saucepan of salted water to the boil. Add the pasta, stir once and boil for 10-12 minutes until tender. Drain well.

2 Meanwhile make the sauce. Chop up the butter and place it in a small pan with the cheese. Heat very gently until the cheese has melted, then add the cream and bring to a simmer, stirring lightly. Add the brandy and all but 1 tablespoon of the nuts. Heat through, taste and add pepper, and salt if necessary.

3 Divide the pasta between warmed serving plates. Pour the sauce over the pasta and sprinkle with pepper and the remaining nuts. Serve immediately.

SHELLS WITH THREE CHEESE SAUCE

SERVES 4

Serve this unashamedly rich pasta sauce with a salad of bitter leaves, such as frisée and radicchio.

350 g (12 oz) pasta shells
150 ml (¼ pint) single cream
75 g (3 oz) dolcelatte cheese, chopped
125 g (4 oz) mozzarella cheese, finely chopped
50 g (2 oz) freshly grated Parmesan cheese
25 g (1 oz) butter
1 tablespoon snipped chives
1 tablespoon chopped parsley
pepper to taste
parsley sprigs to garnish

1 Bring a large saucepan of salted water to the boil. Add the pasta, stir once and boil for 10-12 minutes until tender.

2 Preheat the grill to high. Drain the pasta well, then return to the pan. Add the cream, dolcelatte, mozzarella and half of the Parmesan. Stir in the butter, herbs and pepper and heat through gently until the cheeses are starting to melt.

3 Transfer the mixture to a warmed ovenproof serving dish and sprinkle with the remaining Parmesan. Place under the grill for a few minutes until golden brown. Serve immediately, garnished with parsley.

GNOCCHI WITH SAGE & PROSCIUTTO

SERVES 4

500 g (1 lb) medium-sized floury potatoes
salt and pepper to taste
150 g (5 oz) plain flour
1 egg, beaten

SAUCE
8-10 sage leaves, chopped
150 ml (¼ pint) single cream
125 g (4 oz) frozen broad beans, cooked
25 g (1 oz) prosciutto, thinly sliced

TO SERVE
freshly grated Parmesan cheese

1. Cook the potatoes in their skins in boiling salted water until tender, about 20-25 minutes; drain. When cool enough to handle, peel off the skins and mash the potatoes. Add salt, pepper, flour and egg; mix well.

2. Divide the dough in half and form each into a long sausage shape on a lightly floured surface. Cut into 2.5 cm (1 inch) lengths and mark each by rolling along the prongs of a fork.

3. Place all the ingredients for the sauce in a small pan and simmer gently for a few minutes.

4. Bring a large pan of salted water to the boil. Add the gnocchi and simmer for 4-5 minutes, until they float to the surface. Remove with a slotted spoon and divide between warmed dishes. Pour over the sauce and serve with Parmesan.

PASTA WITH CHICKEN LIVER & SAGE SAUCE

SERVES 4

500 g (1 lb) chicken livers, defrosted if frozen
4 tablespoons olive oil
3 shallots, chopped
1 tablespoon chopped sage leaves
2 tablespoons tomato purée
150 ml (¼ pint) beef consommé
150 ml (¼ pint) water
salt and pepper to taste
2 tablespoons brandy
250-350 g (8-12 oz) pasta shells
1 tablespoon dried breadcrumbs
2 tablespoons chopped parsley

1. Rinse and dry the chicken livers, then cut into small pieces. Heat half of the oil in a saucepan, add the shallots and fry gently for 3-4 minutes. Add the sage and chicken livers and cook over a high heat, stirring until the livers are evenly browned.

2. Add the tomato purée, consommé, water, salt, pepper and brandy. Bring to the boil, cover and simmer for 12-15 minutes.

3. Meanwhile bring a large saucepan of salted water to the boil. Add the pasta, stir once and boil for 10-12 minutes until tender; drain.

4. Heat the remaining oil in the pan, add the breadcrumbs and half of the parsley and fry for 1-2 minutes, until crisp. Add the pasta and toss well.

5. Serve the pasta topped with the sauce and sprinkled with the remaining parsley.

PAPPARDELLE WITH SALMON & BROCCOLI

SERVES 4

250 g (8 oz) pappardelle
250 g (8 oz) broccoli florets
25 g (1 oz) butter
1 tablespoon sunflower oil
1 small leek, sliced
1 teaspoon chopped fresh root ginger
250 g (8 oz) skinned salmon fillet, cubed
150 ml (¼ pint) dry white wine
salt and pepper to taste
3 tablespoons fromage frais
snipped chives to garnish

1 Bring a large pan of salted water to the boil. Add the pasta, stir once and boil for 10-12 minutes until tender.

2 Meanwhile make the sauce. Parcook the broccoli in boiling salted water for 2 minutes; drain. Heat the butter and oil in a saucepan, add the leek and ginger and fry, stirring, for 1 minute. Add the broccoli and salmon and stir around gently. Add the wine and seasoning. Bring to the boil, then cover and simmer for 2-3 minutes, until the salmon is tender.

3 Lower the heat and stir in the fromage frais, a spoonful at a time. Taste and adjust seasoning if necessary.

4 Drain the pasta and mix with the sauce. Serve sprinkled with chives.

PASTA WITH SPICED PRAWNS & CAULIFLOWER

SERVES 4

A deliciously different winter dish.

250 g (8 oz) pasta twists
5 tablespoons sunflower oil
2 cloves garlic, chopped
1 teaspoon cumin seeds
1 teaspoon mustard seeds
250 g (8 oz) cauliflower florets
½ red pepper, seeded and finely chopped
250 g (8 oz) peeled prawns
1 teaspoon paprika
salt to taste
1 teaspoon sesame oil

1 Bring a large pan of salted water to the boil. Add the pasta, stir once and boil for 10-12 minutes until tender. Drain well.

2 Meanwhile, heat the oil in a large frying pan or wok. Add the garlic, cumin and mustard seeds and stir-fry for 1 minute. Add the cauliflower and stir-fry for a further 1-2 minutes until the cauliflower begins to colour. Lower the heat, cover and cook for 5 minutes, stirring occasionally.

3 Add the red pepper, prawns, paprika and salt. Stir well, then cook, covered, for a further 2-3 minutes.

4 Just before serving, add the drained pasta, drizzle in the sesame oil and toss together.

PASTA SPIRALS WITH PORK MEATBALLS

SERVES 4

Make these tasty meatballs in quantity for feeding a
crowd, or freeze some for unexpected guests.

MEATBALLS
500 g (1 lb) minced pork
grated rind of ½ lemon
25 g (1 oz) wholemeal breadcrumbs
1 teaspoon soy sauce
1 egg, beaten
salt and pepper to taste
2 tablespoons olive oil

SAUCE
2 cloves garlic, peeled
1 onion, roughly chopped
2 carrots, roughly chopped
2 sticks celery, roughly chopped
1 red pepper, cored, seeded and roughly chopped
2 teaspoons dried oregano
397 g (14 oz) can chopped tomatoes
150 ml (¼ pint) vegetable stock
1 tablespoon lemon juice
250-350 g (8-12 oz) pasta spirals
1 tablespoon chopped parsley

TO GARNISH
parsley sprigs

1 To prepare the meatballs, put the pork, lemon
rind, breadcrumbs, soy sauce, egg, salt and
pepper into a bowl and mix together, using your
hands, until evenly blended. Shape the mixture into
about 30 small balls.

2 Heat 1 tablespoon of the oil in a saucepan, add
the meatballs and fry for about 5 minutes until
lightly browned. Remove from the pan using a slotted
spoon and transfer to a plate. Drain off all but
1 tablespoon of the oil from the pan.

3 To make the sauce, place the garlic, onion,
carrots, celery and red pepper in a food
processor or blender and work until finely chopped.
Add to the pan and cook, stirring, for 2-3 minutes.
Add the oregano, chopped tomatoes, stock, lemon
juice, salt and pepper and bring to the boil.

4 Return the meatballs to the pan and simmer,
covered, for 15 minutes.

5 Meanwhile cook the pasta. Bring a large
saucepan of salted water to the boil. Add the
pasta spirals, stir once and boil for 10-12 minutes until
tender. Drain well and return to the pan. Add the
parsley and remaining 1 tablespoon oil; toss well.

6 Serve the pasta topped with the meatballs in
sauce, and garnished with parsley.

STIR FRIED FENNEL, PEPPERS & WALNUTS

SERVES 4

Serve this tasty stir fry with fish and chicken dishes.

3 tablespoons groundnut oil
1 clove garlic, crushed
1 large fennel bulb, thinly sliced
1 red pepper, cored, seeded and cut into strips
1 yellow pepper, cored, seeded and thinly sliced
4 spring onions, diagonally sliced
50 g (2 oz) walnut pieces
salt and pepper to taste

SAUCE
5 tablespoons chicken stock or water
2 tablespoons light soy sauce
1 teaspoon wine vinegar
1 teaspoon cornflour
pinch of five-spice powder

1. Mix together all the sauce ingredients in a bowl to a smooth paste and set aside.

2. Heat the oil in a wok. Add the garlic, fennel and peppers and stir fry for 2 minutes. Add the spring onions and the walnuts and stir fry for a few seconds.

3. Pour in the sauce mixture, stirring until thickened. Cover and cook over a low heat for 2 minutes. Season and serve at once.

RATATOUILLE

SERVES 6-8

Stir frying is an ideal way to cook substantial servings of this traditional French vegetable dish. Serve it hot as an accompaniment, or cold as a starter or side salad.

1 aubergine, sliced
1 teaspoon salt
3 tablespoons virgin olive oil
2 onions, sliced
2 cloves garlic, crushed
1 red pepper, cored, seeded and thinly sliced
1 green pepper, cored, seeded and thinly sliced
250 g (8 oz) courgettes, sliced
350 g (12 oz) tomatoes, skinned and chopped
1 tablespoon chopped parsley
2 teaspoons chopped thyme
salt and pepper to taste

1. Rinse the aubergine and place in a colander. Sprinkle with the salt and leave to stand for 20 minutes to remove the bitter juices. Rinse thoroughly to remove the salt and drain.

2. Heat the oil in a wok or large frying pan. Add the onions and garlic and stir fry over a medium heat for 3-4 minutes.

3. Add all the remaining ingredients and stir fry for 3 minutes, then cover and cook over a low heat for about 12 minutes until the vegetables are tender. Adjust the seasoning.

ABOVE: RATATOUILLE *BELOW:* STIR FRIED FENNEL, PEPPERS & WALNUTS

SPINACH & HERB EGGAH

SERVES 4

This is a Middle Eastern omelette. As a variation, try a filling of diced cooked chicken flavoured with spices and pine nuts.

6 eggs
2 leeks, finely chopped
125 g (4 oz) frozen chopped spinach, defrosted and squeezed dry
5 spring onions, chopped
3 tablespoons chopped parsley
3 tablespoons chopped dill or coriander
75 g (3 oz) chopped walnuts
salt and pepper to taste
15 g (½ oz) butter

TO SERVE
coriander sprigs
cherry tomatoes
Greek-style yogurt

1 Preheat oven to 180°C (350°F/Gas 4).

2 Beat the eggs in a large bowl. Stir in the leeks, spinach, spring onions, herbs, walnuts and seasoning.

3 Grease a 25 cm (10 inch) round ovenproof dish with the butter and pour in the mixture. Bake for 30 minutes, covering with foil if the top browns too quickly.

4 Serve warm or cold, cut into wedges. Garnish with coriander and tomatoes, and serve with yogurt.

FRITTATA

SERVES 4

This Italian baked omelette is good served hot or cold. Cut into fingers, it makes perfect party food.

4 tablespoons olive oil
1 large onion, sliced
1 red pepper, cored, seeded and sliced
1 green pepper, cored, seeded and sliced
2 courgettes, sliced
3 cloves garlic, thinly sliced
4 eggs, beaten
salt and pepper to taste
90 ml (3 fl oz) milk
basil leaves to garnish

1 Preheat oven to 200°C (400°F/Gas 6).

2 Heat the olive oil in a frying pan. Add the onion and peppers and cook until soft. Transfer to an oiled 20-23cm (8-9 inch) ovenproof dish, using a slotted spoon.

3 Add the courgettes to the frying pan and sauté until tender and golden. Add to the onion and peppers.

4 Sauté the garlic slices in the frying pan until softened. Add to the vegetables.

5 Season the eggs with salt and pepper and stir in the milk. Pour over the vegetables and mix lightly to distribute evenly.

6 Dot the top with a few basil leaves, reserving some for garnish. Bake for 25-30 minutes, until set and golden brown.

7 Garnish with the remaining basil and serve hot or cold, cut into squares.

GRILLED AUBERGINE SLICES

SERVES 4

These are like mini pizzas – using large aubergine slices for the bases instead of dough. They make an excellent starter too.

1 large aubergine
olive oil for brushing
2×150 g (5 oz) mozzarella cheeses
8-12 tablespoons passata
pepper to taste
1 tablespoon chopped oregano
oregano sprigs to garnish

1 Preheat grill to medium and preheat oven to 200°C (400°F/Gas 6).

2 Cut the aubergine into 8-12 slices, each 1 cm (½ inch) thick. Brush both sides with olive oil. Grill for about 3 minutes on each side until golden.

3 Cut the mozzarella into as many slices as you have aubergine and place on top of the aubergine. Top each with a tablespoon of passata, a little olive oil and a sprinkling of pepper. Bake for about 5 minutes until the mozzarella has melted.

4 Sprinkle with the chopped oregano and serve warm, garnished with oregano sprigs.

BRUSCHETTA

SERVES 4

This Italian garlic bread calls for the best olive oil – preferably first pressed – for maximum flavour. Use plum tomatoes if possible.

4 ripe tomatoes
8 thick slices of crusty white bread
4 cloves garlic
6 tablespoons quality olive oil
salt and pepper to taste

TO GARNISH
torn basil leaves
olive slices

1 Preheat the grill to high.

2 Immerse the tomatoes in boiling water for 30 seconds, then drain and plunge into cold water. Carefully peel away the skins. Cut the tomatoes into quarters and discard the seeds. Chop roughly.

3 Toast the bread on both sides until golden brown. Rub one side of the hot toast with the cut garlic.

4 Place the toasts, garlic side up, on a serving dish and drizzle with the olive oil.

5 Pile the chopped tomato on to the toast and sprinkle with salt and pepper. Garnish with basil and olive slices. Serve immediately.

SPICED CAULIFLOWER, SPINACH & POTATO

SERVES 4-6

Serve with simply grilled chicken or meat, or as part of an Indian meal.

500 g (1 lb) small new potatoes, halved
½ cauliflower, divided into florets
3 tablespoons olive oil
25 g (1 oz) butter
1 clove garlic, crushed
1 large red chilli, sliced and seeded
1 teaspoon cumin seeds, lightly crushed
1 teaspoon coriander seeds, lightly crushed
1 teaspoon mustard seeds, lightly crushed
1 teaspoon garam masala
pinch of turmeric
125 g (4 oz) spinach, finely shredded
salt and pepper to taste

1 Parboil the new potatoes in boiling salted water for 5-6 minutes, then drain.

2 Meanwhile, in a separate pan parboil the cauliflower for 3-4 minutes. Drain thoroughly.

3 Heat the oil and butter in a wok or large frying pan. Add the garlic, chilli and spices and stir fry for a few seconds. Add the potatoes and cauliflower and stir fry for about 4 minutes, until the vegetables are just tender.

4 Add the spinach to the wok and toss lightly to mix. Leave on the heat just long enough for the spinach to wilt. Season and serve immediately.

FIVE SPICED CHINESE LEAF

SERVES 4-6

This tasty stir fry featuring light Chinese leaf and crisp water chestnuts makes a good accompaniment. You can use pak choi or Chinese cabbage instead of the more lettuce-like Chinese leaf.

2 tablespoons groundnut oil
1 teaspoon sesame oil
2.5 cm (1 inch) piece fresh root ginger, grated
large pinch of five-spice powder
215 g (7 oz) can water chestnuts, drained and sliced
2 tablespoons sherry or sake (rice wine)
1 tablespoon soy sauce
½ teaspoon soft light brown sugar
1 head Chinese leaf, roughly torn
salt and pepper to taste

TO GARNISH
coriander leaves

1 Heat the oils in a wok. Add the ginger, five-spice powder and water chestnuts and stir fry for 2 minutes. Stir in the sherry or sake, soy sauce and sugar.

2 Add the Chinese leaf to the wok and stir fry for about 2 minutes, until the leaves are slightly wilted but the white stalks are still crisp. Season with salt and pepper and serve at once, garnished with coriander leaves.

SPAGHETTI VEGETABLES WITH ALMONDS

SERVES 4

Shoe-string lengths of carrot, parsnip and courgette with a buttery glaze and toasted almond flakes make an elegant, colourful vegetable accompaniment. Sometimes I use a leek in place of one of the vegetables listed below.

3 medium carrots
2 parsnips
2 courgettes
15 g (½ oz) flaked almonds
2 tablespoons olive oil
small knob of butter
½ teaspoon soft light brown sugar
1 tablespoon lemon juice
salt and pepper to taste

1 Slice the vegetables lengthwise, then cut into long thin julienne or 'spaghetti'.

2 Place the almonds in a wok over a moderate heat and stir until evenly browned; remove and set aside.

3 Heat the oil in the wok, add the vegetables and stir fry for 3 minutes until just tender. Add the butter, sugar and lemon juice and cook, stirring, for 1-2 minutes until glazed.

4 Season with salt and pepper and transfer to a warmed serving dish. Sprinkle with the almonds to serve.

PEPPERS & PERNOD

SERVES 4

Multi-coloured peppers, flavoured with aniseed and fresh basil, are excellent with fish and chicken dishes. This dish may also be chilled and served as a salad accompaniment.

1 each red, green and yellow pepper
2 tablespoons virgin olive oil
3 tablespoons chopped basil
4 tablespoons Pernod, Ouzo or other aniseed liqueur
salt and pepper to taste

TO GARNISH
basil leaves

1 Halve, core, seed and thinly slice the peppers.

2 Heat the oil in a wok or large pan. Add the peppers and stir fry for 3 minutes.

3 Add the basil and Pernod, Ouzo or aniseed liqueur. Cover and cook over a medium heat for 3 minutes, stirring once. Season with salt and pepper. Transfer to a warmed serving dish and garnish with basil leaves to serve.

FRENCH BEAN & MUSHROOM STIR FRY

SERVES 4

Cloud ear mushrooms are not essential to this stir fry, but they add texture. You can buy them dried from Chinese supermarkets, but use sparingly as they grow to huge proportions when soaked!

3 dried cloud ear mushrooms (optional)
3 tablespoons groundnut oil
½ clove garlic, crushed
2.5 cm (1 inch) piece fresh root ginger, grated
1 small leek, thinly sliced
250 g (8 oz) French beans
175 g (6 oz) small open cup mushrooms
2 tablespoons yellow bean sauce or paste
1 tablespoon light soy sauce
pepper to taste

1 If using cloud ear mushrooms, place in a small bowl, cover with boiling water and leave to soak for 20 minutes. Drain, reserving 5 tablespoons liquid. Cut the mushrooms into bite-sized pieces.

2 Heat the oil in a wok. Add the garlic, ginger, leek and French beans, and stir fry for 2 minutes. Add all the mushrooms and stir fry for 1-2 minutes more.

3 Add the yellow bean paste and soy sauce, together with the reserved mushrooms liquid or 5 tablespoons water. Cover and simmer for 2-3 minutes. Season with pepper and serve immediately.

SWEET & SOUR BEANS

SERVES 4

A delicious combination of mixed beans and tomatoes in a light sweet and sour sauce. If short-sprouted beans are not available, use bean sprouts instead.

3 tablespoons groundnut oil
½ clove garlic, crushed
250 g (8 oz) green beans, halved
215 g (7 oz) can red kidney beans, drained
4 tomatoes, skinned and quartered
3 spring onions, shredded
75 g (3 oz) short-sprouted beans
salt and pepper to taste

SAUCE
3 tablespoons light soy sauce
3 tablespoons wine vinegar
3 tablespoons sherry
1 tablespoon clear honey
2 tablespoons soft light brown sugar
6 tablespoons water
1 teaspoon cornflour

1 Mix together all the sauce ingredients in a bowl to a smooth paste and set aside.

2 Heat the oil in a wok. Add the garlic and green beans and stir fry for 1 minute. Add the remaining ingredients and stir fry for 2 minutes.

3 Pour in the sauce mixture, stirring until thickened. Cover and cook gently for 2 minutes. Season with salt and pepper and serve at once.

BABY CORNS WRAPPED IN BACON

MAKES 16

Another snack which works well as a party canapé – and equally successfully as a children's treat!

16 baby corn cobs
8 slices streaky bacon, derinded
olive oil for brushing

DIP
90 ml (3 fl oz) mayonnaise
1 tablespoon tomato ketchup
squeeze of lemon juice
few drops of Tabasco
salt and pepper to taste

TO GARNISH
parsley sprigs

1 Cook the baby corn in boiling salted water for 3-4 minutes. Plunge into cold water and drain. Dry on kitchen paper.

2 Preheat grill to medium. Halve each bacon rasher lengthwise and twist a strip around each corn cob, leaving the tip exposed.

3 Brush with a little oil and grill, turning, until the bacon is slightly crispy.

4 For the dip, mix together the mayonnaise, tomato ketchup, lemon juice, Tabasco and seasoning in a bowl.

5 Serve the corns warm, garnished with parsley and accompanied by the tomato dip.

SPRING ROLLS

MAKES 6

1 tablespoon vegetable oil
500 g (1 lb) frozen stir-fry mixed vegetables
1 teaspoon salt
1 teaspoon sugar
1 teaspoon light soy sauce
1 teaspoon dark soy sauce
1 teaspoon sesame oil
3 large sheets filo pastry, each about 42×30 cm
    (17×12 inches)
oil for brushing
coriander sprigs to garnish
chilli oil to serve

1 Preheat oven to 200°C (400°F/Gas 6).

2 Heat the oil in a wok or large frying pan. When very hot, add the vegetables and stir-fry for about 5 minutes. Drain off any excess liquid. Add the salt, sugar, soy sauces and sesame oil. Set aside.

3 Cut the filo sheets in half lengthwise to give 6 strips. Brush 1 strip lightly with oil and place 2 tablespoons of the stir-fried vegetables at one end, leaving a 5 cm (2 inch) border at the edge. Fold this over the vegetables and fold in 1 cm (½ inch) of the sides of the pastry. Roll up like a cigar and place on a lightly oiled baking sheet. Repeat with the remaining filo pastry and filling.

4 Brush the rolls lightly with oil and bake for about 20 minutes, until golden.

5 Garnish with coriander and serve with chilli oil for dipping.

STUFFED SQUASH

SERVES 4

Choose small even-sized summer squashes, such as round courgettes or patty pans.

8 squashes, each about 175 g (6 oz)
salt and pepper to taste
50 g (2 oz) butter
1 small onion, finely chopped
1 clove garlic, crushed
250 g (8 oz) lean beef, minced
230 g (8 oz) can chopped tomatoes
1 tablespoon chopped fresh root ginger
½ teaspoon ground cinnamon
1 tablespoon raisins
1 tablespoon pine nuts

1 Cook the squashes in boiling salted water until tender; 15-20 minutes, depending on size. Alternatively, cook in the microwave for 6-8 minutes. Drain.

2 Slice off the tops of the squash for lids. Scoop out the flesh, leaving 5 mm (¼ inch) thick shells. Chop the flesh.

3 Preheat oven to 200°C (400°F/Gas 6).

4 Melt the butter in a pan, add the onion and garlic and cook until softened.

5 Add the meat and fry, stirring, until browned. Add the tomatoes, ginger, seasoning, cinnamon, raisins and nuts; simmer for 10-15 minutes. Stir in the chopped squash.

6 Fill the squashes with stuffing, replace the lids and place in a roasting tin, containing 2.5 cm (1 inch) water. Bake for 10 minutes, until hot. Serve with Greek yogurt and a side salad.

GNOCCHI WITH ROCKET SAUCE

SERVES 4

Try this Italian favourite, made simpler by using instant mashed potato.

125 g (4 oz) instant mashed potato
salt and pepper to taste
grated nutmeg to taste
125 g (4 oz) plain flour, sifted
60 ml (2 fl oz) white wine
20 g (¾ oz) rocket, finely chopped
150 ml (5 fl oz) double cream
25 g (1 oz) butter
2 tablespoons freshly grated Parmesan cheese
rocket leaves to garnish

1 Cook potato according to the quick method packet instructions. Add seasoning and nutmeg. Let cool for a few minutes. Add the flour and mix until smooth.

2 With floured hands, shape the potato mixture into 2 cm (¾ inch) thick rolls. Cut into 2.5 cm (1 inch) lengths. Mark with the back of a fork.

3 Bring a large pan of salted water to the boil and cook the gnocchi, in batches of 10, for about 10 seconds. Lift out with a slotted spoon and place in a warm dish.

4 Simmer the wine until reduced by half. Add the rocket and cream and boil for 3 minutes, until slightly thickened. Off the heat, whisk in the butter and seasoning.

5 Pour the sauce over the gnocchi and sprinkle with Parmesan. Garnish with rocket leaves and serve immediately.

MUSHROOM LASAGNE

SERVES 4-6

15 g (½ oz) dried porcini mushrooms
2 tablespoons olive oil
2 shallots, chopped
1 tablespoon tomato purée
2 tablespoons chopped parsley
salt and pepper to taste
500 g (1 lb) chestnut mushrooms, sliced
600 ml (1 pint) milk
40 g (1½ oz) butter
40 g (1½ oz) plain flour
250-300 g (8-10 oz) fresh lasagne
50 g (2 oz) freshly grated Parmesan cheese

1 Soak the porcini in 300 ml (½ pint) hot water for 30 minutes then drain; strain the soaking liquid and reserve. Slice the mushrooms thinly.

2 Preheat oven to 200°C (400°F/Gas 6). Heat the oil in a pan and fry the shallots until softened. Add the porcini, reserved liquid, tomato purée, parsley and seasoning. Simmer for 15 minutes, then add the fresh mushrooms and cook for 5 minutes.

3 Warm the milk. Melt the butter in a pan, add the flour and cook for 1 minute. Whisk in the milk then cook, whisking, until the sauce is smooth and thickened. Add seasoning.

4 Layer the ingredients in a buttered shallow oblong dish in the following order: sauce, lasagne, mushroom, lasagne, mushroom, lasagne, sauce; sprinkling Parmesan over each layer. Bake for 15-20 minutes, until golden brown. Serve with a salad.

RIGATONI FIORENTINA

SERVES 4

This dish is similar to one served at my favourite Italian café.

1 quantity fresh tomato sauce (page 14)
salt and pepper to taste
250 g (8 oz) rigatoni
125 g (4 oz) spinach leaves
50 g (2 oz) gruyère cheese, grated
2 tablespoons freshly grated Parmesan cheese
1 tablespoon olive oil

1 Make the tomato sauce and keep warm. Bring a large saucepan of salted water to the boil. Add the pasta, stir once and boil for 10-12 minutes until tender.

2 Meanwhile cook the spinach in the minimum of water for about 5 minutes, until tender. Drain thoroughly and chop roughly. Stir into the tomato sauce.

3 Preheat the grill to high. Drain the rigatoni, add to the sauce and mix well. Transfer to a warmed oiled ovenproof dish. Sprinkle with the gruyère and Parmesan and drizzle with the oil. Place under the hot grill for 2-3 minutes, until golden and bubbling. Serve immediately.

ONIONS IN HORSERADISH CREAM

SERVES 4-6

This original stir fry of pearl, red and spring onions with horseradish and a touch of cream is delicious served with seafood and smoked fish, sausages, red meat and chicken. If pearl onions with their characteristic pink-tinged skins are not available, use tiny button onions instead.

250 g (8 oz) pearl onions
1 red onion
6 spring onions
3 tablespoons groundnut oil
2 tablespoons lemon juice
2 tablespoons creamed horseradish
3 tablespoons single cream
salt and pepper to taste

1 Top and tail the pearl onions. Cut the red onion into wedges and separate layers into petals. Cut spring onions diagonally into 5 cm (2 inch) lengths.

2 Heat the oil in a wok or large frying pan. Add the pearl onions and stir fry for 2 minutes. Add the red onion and spring onions and stir fry for a further 2 minutes.

3 Add the lemon juice and creamed horseradish to the wok with 2-3 tablespoons water. Cover and cook for 2 minutes. Stir in the cream and salt and pepper. Serve at once.

BABY ONIONS WITH BACON

SERVES 4-6

A delicious accompaniment for grilled and roast meats. For a richer version, substitute some of the stock with white wine or dry vermouth.

125 g (4 oz) back bacon rashers, derinded and
  diced
15 g (½ oz) butter
24 small button onions (approximately)
150 ml (¼ pint) light stock or water
4 tablespoons double cream
1 teaspoon chopped thyme
1 teaspoon cornflour
salt and pepper to taste

TO GARNISH
thyme sprigs

1 Cook the bacon in a wok or large frying pan, without additional fat, for 1-2 minutes, until just crisp. Remove with a slotted spoon and set aside.

2 Add the butter to the pan with the onions. Stir fry for 2 minutes, then add the stock or water and return the bacon to the pan. Cover and cook over a medium heat for 5-7 minutes, until the onions are tender. Stir in the cream and thyme.

3 Mix the cornflour to a paste with a little cold water, then add to the pan and stir until thickened. Season with salt and pepper and serve at once, garnished with thyme.

ABOVE: ONIONS IN HORSERADISH CREAM *BELOW*: BABY ONIONS WITH BACON

SPICED BANANAS WITH RUM

SERVES 4

For an indulgent dessert, serve these delicious bananas with whipped cream or ice cream and brandy snaps. Less sinful people may prefer them with Greek-style yogurt or smetana!

4 large bananas
juice of 1 lemon
40 g (1½ oz) butter
4 tablespoons soft light brown sugar
½ teaspoon ground mixed spice
5 tablespoons dark rum
½ teaspoon cornflour
finely pared and shredded rind and juice of 1 orange
orange slices to decorate

1 Cut the bananas diagonally into 5 cm (2 inch) lengths. Toss them in the lemon juice to prevent discoloration, then drain well.

2 Heat the butter in a wok or large frying pan. Add the bananas, sugar and spice and stir fry gently for about 2 minutes until beginning to soften. Stir in the rum and cook for a further 1 minute until the bananas are hot and tender.

3 Carefully transfer the bananas to a warmed serving plate using a slotted spoon, leaving the juices in the pan.

4 Mix the cornflour to a paste with the orange juice. Add to the pan with the shredded orange rind and cook, stirring, for 1 minute until thickened. Pour over the bananas and serve immediately, decorated with orange slices.

CARAMELIZED APPLES & PEARS

SERVES 4

I like to serve this dessert with dollops of cream, crème fraîche or thick yogurt – sprinkled with ground cinnamon.

1 lemon
2 dessert apples
3 firm pears
50 g (2 oz) butter
2-3 tablespoons brandy
2-3 tablespoons demerara sugar

1 Using a zester, finely pare the rind from half of the lemon in strips. Shred finely and set aside. Squeeze the juice from the lemon.

2 Peel, halve and core the apples and pears, then cut each into thick wedges. Toss in the lemon juice to prevent discoloration, then drain well on kitchen paper.

3 Heat the butter in a wok or large frying pan, add the fruit and stir fry over a high heat for 2-3 minutes until the apples and pears are golden brown; take care to avoid burning.

4 Sprinkle with the brandy and sugar. Continue to stir fry for about 3 minutes until the fruit is glazed with caramel. Stir in the lemon zest.

5 Serve hot, with cream, crème fraîche or yogurt.

EXOTIC FRUIT STIR FRY

SERVES 4

Exotic fruits such as star fruit, kumquats and pineapple stir fry rather well, staying intact as long as you are fairly gentle. Serve this dessert hot or cold with cream, fromage frais or yogurt, or with melt-in-the-mouth meringues.

40 g (1½ oz) butter
175 g (6 oz) kumquats, halved
2 star fruit, sliced
1 mango, peeled, stoned and sliced
½ small pineapple, peeled, cored and cubed
25-50 g (1-2 oz) soft light brown sugar
juice of 1 lemon
finely grated rind and juice of 1 lime
½ teaspoon cornflour
4 tablespoons Marsala or other sweet wine
edible flowers to decorate (optional)

1 Melt the butter in a wok. Add the fruits and stir fry for 3 minutes. Add the sugar, lemon juice, lime rind and juice, and cook for 2 minutes until the sugar is dissolved.

2 Mix the cornflour to a paste with the Marsala, then add to the wok and cook, stirring gently, until thickened. Serve hot or chilled, sprinkled with edible flowers if available.

CHERRIES IN COINTREAU

SERVES 4

These sweet black cherries in a cointreau-flavoured sauce can be served hot or chilled with ice cream, cream or yogurt and crisp dessert biscuits. I leave the cherries whole so they hold their shape during cooking, but you may prefer to stone them first.

500 g (1 lb) ripe black cherries
25 g (1 oz) caster sugar
1 cinnamon stick
finely grated rind and juice of 1 orange
5 tablespoons cointreau
1 teaspoon cornflour

1 Place the cherries in a wok or large saucepan with the sugar, cinnamon, orange rind and juice and 125 ml (4 fl oz) water. Cook, stirring, over a medium heat for 2-3 minutes until the sugar is dissolved. Lower the heat and simmer for 5 minutes or until the cherries are quite soft but not collapsing; the timing will depend upon the ripeness of the cherries.

2 Stir in the cointreau and heat through. Remove the cherries, using a slotted spoon, and place in a warmed serving dish.

3 Mix the cornflour to a paste with 1 tablespoon cold water. Add to the pan and cook, stirring, until thickened. Pour over the hot cherries. Serve immediately or allow to cool and chill before serving.

PEAR & APRICOT COMPOTE

SERVES 4

A delicious compote, subtly flavoured with vanilla and topped with pistachio nuts.

TOPPING
15 g (½ oz) butter
25 g (1 oz) shelled pistachio nuts, chopped
finely grated rind of ½ lemon
1 tablespoon caster sugar

COMPOTE
250 g (8 oz) dried pears
250 g (8 oz) no-soak dried apricots
25 g (1 oz) caster sugar
juice of 1 lemon
1 vanilla pod
150 ml (¼ pint) sweet dessert wine

1 For the topping, melt the butter in a small frying pan, add the nuts and fry gently for 2 minutes or until just beginning to brown. Stir in the lemon rind and sugar. Remove from the heat and set aside.

2 Place all the ingredients for the compote in a pan with 5 tablespoons water. Cook gently, stirring until the sugar is dissolved, then cover and allow to simmer for 20 minutes, until the fruit is tender. Remove the lid and boil briskly until the liquid is reduced to a thin syrup. Discard the vanilla.

3 Serve the compote hot or chilled, sprinkled with the pistachio topping and accompanied by cream or yogurt.

PINEAPPLE WITH COCONUT CREAM

SERVES 4

Stem ginger preserved in syrup is available in jars from most supermarkets. Here it is combined with pina colada flavours – pineapple, coconut and cream.

40 g (1½ oz) butter
1 large pineapple, peeled, cored and sliced
3 pieces preserved stem ginger, thinly sliced
2 tablespoons demerara sugar
pinch of ground cinnamon
¼ teaspoon finely grated lemon rind
2 tablespoons white rum
25 g (1 oz) creamed coconut, in pieces
150 ml (¼ pint) double cream
shredded lemon zest and mint sprigs to decorate

1 Melt the butter in a wok. Add the pineapple and ginger and stir fry for 4 minutes. Add the sugar, cinnamon, lemon rind and rum and cook for 2-3 minutes until the sugar is dissolved and the pineapple is tender. Transfer the pineapple and ginger to a serving plate, using a slotted spoon.

2 Boil the cooking juices in the pan until reduced to about 3 tablespoons. Lower the heat, then add the creamed coconut and cook, stirring, until melted. Remove from the heat and leave until cold. Softly whip the cream and fold in the coconut mixture.

3 Spoon the coconut cream on top of the pineapple and sprinkle with the lemon zest. Decorate with mint sprigs.

APRICOTS WITH HONEY & ALMONDS

SERVES 4-6

You can serve this dish hot or cold, simply with yogurt or fromage frais. Illustrated on page 126.

40 g (1½ oz) split blanched almonds
25 g (1 oz) butter
500 g (1 lb) apricots, halved and stoned
½ teaspoon ground cinnamon
3 tablespoons brandy
3 tablespoons clear honey
mint sprigs to decorate

1 Stir the almonds in a large frying pan or wok over moderate heat until golden brown. Add the butter, apricots and cinnamon and stir fry for 3 minutes.

2 Stir in the brandy and honey and continue cooking for 2 minutes, or until the apricots are just soft.

3 Serve hot or cold, decorated with mint.

SCENTED RHUBARB

SERVES 4

Cardamom adds a wonderful subtle fragrance to this sharp fruit. Serve well chilled with a dollop of clotted cream, mascarpone cheese or thick cream and crisp dessert biscuits. Illustrated on page 124.

750 g (1½ lb) rhubarb
50 g (2 oz) caster sugar
5 green or white cardamom pods
150 ml (¼ pint) sweet dessert wine
mint sprigs to decorate

1 Cut the rhubarb into 4 cm (1½ inch) lengths and place in a large frying pan or sauté pan with the sugar. Cook, over a medium heat, stirring occasionally, for 4-5 minutes until the sugar is dissolved and the pink juices run from the fruit.

2 Meanwhile, crack open the cardamom pods and take out the seeds; discard the pods. Crush the seeds, using a pestle and mortar or rolling pin.

3 Add the crushed cardamom seeds and dessert wine to the pan and bring to the boil. Lower the heat and simmer for 4-5 minutes until the rhubarb is soft but still holding its shape; do not overcook or the fruit will collapse to a pulp.

4 Allow to cool, then chill before serving. Decorate with mint sprigs.

INDEX